STAND

seeking the WAY of God

ALEX McFARLAND

Colorado Springs, Colorado

Stand: Seeking the Way of God
Copyright © 2009 by Alex McFarland
All rights reserved. International copyright secured.

A Focus on the Family **book**

Editor: Marianne Hering
Contributing writer: Michael Ross
Cover design: Erik M. Peterson
Cover photo of road signs copyright © by iStockphoto.
All rights reserved.

ISBN-10: 1-58997-484-0
ISBN-13: 978-1-58997-484-5

Dedicated to
Peace and Caleb

CONTENTS

INTRODUCTION

be a dreamer

We all have dreams. Some are burning passions that define our identities; others are secret yearnings we lock away in our hearts.

I once met a young man who dreamed of becoming an Olympic swimmer. At the age of 10, he pursued the sport with such discipline that he was recruited by one of the nation's best trainers. But after years of diligent preparation, his dream changed. During his teen years he set his sights on the United States Air Force Academy, believing that God was calling him to be a pilot and an officer.

Did he give up his Olympic dreams? Yes. But the Lord had given him a passion for swimming so that he could develop discipline and perseverance. God replaced one dream with an even bigger vision.

I experienced that in my own life. Long before I committed my life to Christ, I wanted to be a rock star. I learned to play the guitar and spent every spare moment practicing. I imagined myself standing onstage with the Beach Boys! During college I performed in bands, and one of my proudest moments was when I earned enough cash playing gigs to buy my first Rickenbacker guitar—an instrument my musical heroes had mastered.

And my dream to jam with the Beach Boys was fulfilled! When the band performed near my college, I was invited to play a song onstage with them. Then, months later, I was offered a job traveling with the band. Amazingly I turned the offer down. Why? Because an even more incredible thing had happened to me: I committed my life to Jesus Christ.

When I became a Christian, my priorities changed. I decided to go to graduate school and earn a degree in apologetics. Although my love for the guitar and for music didn't go away—I still love jamming with friends or playing alone—God birthed a new dream in me: the passion to become a preacher and a writer. The cool thing is, the countless hours I spent practicing and performing had, almost against my will, built qualities in me that have served me well to this day.

You see, when we're young, we have lots of dreams for our future. Sometimes these dreams are naive and driven by whim. (As a kid I wanted to be an astronaut, a soldier, and a cowboy—often all in the same day!) But the process of growing up involves receiving new dreams from God . . . and discarding old ones.

My goal of becoming a preacher and a writer didn't come easily. There were days when I despaired of it ever coming true. But I learned that it didn't matter how many times I got knocked down, as long as I stayed faithful to the Lord and kept getting up each time I got knocked down.

Joseph learned this too. As a boy he had dreams of becoming a leader—and even one day ruling over his brothers. That dream was delayed and deferred, but it never went away. The dream, and the promise of its fulfillment, kept Joseph moving forward even during the darkest times. And, interestingly, being the lord of his brothers wasn't even the most important part of the dream. God gave Joseph only a part of the vision. The dream in God's mind (if I may put it that way) wasn't to make Joseph a ruler but to make his family the seed of the Jewish people. God replaced one dream with another, and the second dream was even bigger than the first.

Here are a couple of questions for you: What do you think God wants to accomplish in your life? Is there a particular dream burning in your heart—a passion that seems to define you? Remember, as you grow, some of your goals will fall by the wayside. Like the young swimmer I described, you may replace your dreams with a better one. That's all part of God's plan!

American author Napoleon Hill once said, "Cherish your visions and dreams, as they are the children of your soul. Visions and dreams are the blueprints of your ultimate achievements."[1]

We don't always know where our dreams will take us, but we can rest assured that God gives us dreams to move us farther down a road He wants us to travel. The ultimate destination of this journey is a mystery at times, but hold tight. In light of God's sovereignty, we can . . .

- *follow* God's revealed will with obedience;
- *wait* on God's concealed will with anticipation;
- *believe* in God's righteous nature with assurance; and
- *trust* in God's complete power with confidence.

There's no doubt about it: The Lord's hand of blessing was firmly on Joseph's life. By faith he overcame tremendous adversity, grew in wisdom, and rose to a position of prominence in Egypt. And through it all he held tightly to his dreams, trusting God's call on his life. Yet Joseph's story is more than a lesson in how to handle hard times. It's an example of spiritual "wait training." Because Joseph waited on the Lord, never once compromising, God rewarded him—and used him to impact future generations for eternity.

> *Destiny? Tomorrow? Truth? All are questions within the reach of the man who knows his source: Jesus.*
> *—Max Lucado,* Grace for the Moment

Joseph set an example through his . . .

- *belief* in God's sovereignty,
- *character* in resisting compromise,
- *vision* for his place in God's kingdom, and
- *leadership* in every circumstance he faced.

Genesis fast facts

- The book of beginnings: creation, man, the sabbath, marriage, sin, sacrifice, nations, God's covenant, music, art, civilizations, languages, and salvation
- Theme: salvation
- Author: Jews and Christians agree that Moses was the writer-compiler of the first five books of the Old Testament—the Pentateuch—yet some scholars argue that different writers from various periods of Israel's history contributed to these works.
- Genesis is divided into 11 sections, each beginning with the word "account".
- The numbers 10, 7, 12, and 40 have symbolic significance in Genesis.
- The subjects and themes of the first three chapters of Genesis are reflected in the last three chapters of Revelation.

THE BEGINNING OF MISERY——AND HOPE

The book of Genesis chronicles everything from sin and evil to shame and cover-up, broken fellowship, erected barriers, attacks on God, and flight from God. It's the story of the fall, out of which C. S. Lewis wrote "has come nearly all that we call human history—money, poverty, ambition, war, prostitution, classes, empire, slavery—the long terrible story of man trying to find something other than God which will make him happy."[2] Yet the message of Genesis is also one of grace—God's grace—

God created all things

"You alone are the LORD. You made the heavens, even the highest heavens, and all their starry host, the earth and all that is on it, the seas and all that is in them. You give life to everything, and the multitudes of heaven worship you" (Nehemiah 9:6).

The weight of historical evidence not only makes it possible to believe in God's existence, it makes it very hard to ignore. Regardless, truth is truth, and God is who He is. All the arm twisting and eloquent speeches in the world can't convince a nonbelieving friend that creation belongs to God. In fact, arm twisting and eloquent speeches aren't exactly God's style. Transforming a hardened heart is the work of God Himself.

and hope. It's the hope that began when God broke our unholy alliance with the Devil.

LET'S TAKE A JOURNEY THROUGH JOSEPH'S LIFE . . .

And gain some insights about seeking the way of God.

The book you're reading isn't merely an academic exercise; it's also a devotional one. The goal is to have a more intimate relationship with the One who gave us the Bible (not to ace a test on Genesis). In other words, I want you to know not only the book but the Author as well—our Lord God, the Creator of all things.

Joseph knew God intimately. And his attitude toward life reminds me of the story of a man who always wrote "Rom. 8:28" every time he signed his name.

Once while staying in a hotel, the man signed the ticket for his meal. The waitress looked at what the man had written and said, "Sir, did you mean to charge this to your room? You can't do that, since we don't have a Room 8:28."

The man smiled and had the opportunity to explain: "In all things God works for the good . . ."

Thousands of years ago, well before Romans 8:28 was written by the apostle Paul, Joseph understood that truth. It's a promise that's available to every Christian today.

> [God] says, . . . "Make your requests known to Me." And so we come in order to know him and to be known by him.
> —R. C. Sproul, Effective Prayer

Joseph teaches us that even though the glory of this world is fleeting and flawed by strife, true fulfillment can be found by intimately knowing, intensely loving, passionately serving, and completely trusting the God of the universe. Eternal peace is at the core of God's gift of salvation.

What's so special about Joseph? Genesis says this ...

1. Joseph had God's blessing:
   The Lord was with Joseph and he prospered. (Genesis 39:2)

   But while Joseph was there in the prison, the Lord was with him; he showed him kindness and granted him favor in the eyes of the prison warden. ... The warden paid no attention to anything under Joseph's care, because the Lord was with Joseph and gave him success in whatever he did. (39:20-21, 23)

2. Joseph had his boss's blessing through God:
   "When his master saw that the Lord was with him and that the Lord gave him success in everything he did, Joseph found favor in his eyes and became his attendant. (Genesis 39:3-4)

   So the warden put Joseph in charge of all those held in the prison, and he was made responsible for all that was done there. (39:22)

   Then Pharaoh said to Joseph, "Since God has made [the dream's interpretation] known to you, there is no one so discerning and wise as you. you shall be in charge of my palace, and all my people are to submit to your orders. only with respect to the throne will I be greater than you." (41:39-40)

3. Joseph was God's dream interpreter:
Now a young Hebrew was there [in prison] with us, a servant of the captain of the guard. we told him our dreams, and he interpreted them for us, giving each man the interpretation of his dream. And things turned out exactly as he interpreted them to us. (Genesis 41:12-13)

"I cannot [interpret your dream]," Joseph replied to Pharaoh, "but God will give Pharaoh the answer he desires." (41:16)

4. Joseph was God's servant:
[Joseph said,] "But God sent me ahead of you to preserve for you a remnant on earth and to save your lives by a great deliverance. so then, it was not you who sent me here, but God." (Genesis 45:7-8)

TIME LINE OF JOSEPH'S LIFE

1770–1764 BC Jacob completes 14 years of work for his father-in-law, Laban, as payment for his wives, Rachel and Leah. Son Joseph is born to Rachel when Jacob is 91. (Genesis 30:22-43; see also 29:14-30)

1764 Jacob and his family return to live in Canaan, to be free of domineering Laban. (Genesis 31)

1763 Jacob wrestles with God by a brook called Jabbok. God changes his name to Israel. (Genesis 32:22-30)

1757 Jacob and his sons move to Bethel, and God renews the covenant there with Jacob. (Genesis 35:1-15)

1734 Benjamin is born to Jacob and Rachel, and Rachel dies in childbirth. (Genesis 35:16-21)

1727 Joseph, age 17, is his father's favorite. In jealousy, his brothers sell Joseph into Egyptian slavery and convince their father that Joseph is dead. (Genesis 37)

1726–1720 Joseph, now a slave of Potiphar, eventually rises to be chief manager over Potiphar's house. (Genesis 39:1-6)

1720 Potiphar's wife accuses Joseph of molesting her, and Joseph is imprisoned. (Genesis 39:7-20)

1720–1716 Joseph is put in charge over the prisoners in the jail. (Genesis 39:21-23)

1716 Pharaoh's baker and cupbearer are imprisoned, and both experience mysterious dreams. Joseph interprets both dreams correctly. (Genesis 40)

1714 Pharaoh dreams a disturbing two-part dream, which no one can interpret. Pharaoh's cupbearer remembers Joseph, who is summoned from prison. Joseph interprets the dream and warns of seven years of plenty followed by seven years of severe famine. Pharaoh elevates Joseph to a ruling position as second in command over all of Egypt. Joseph is age 30. (Genesis 41:1–46)

1714–1707 Joseph presides over the growth and storage of grain throughout all of Egypt. (Genesis 41:46–49)

1707 Harsh famine strikes Egypt and Canaan. Joseph begins to ration out and sell the stored grain. (Genesis 41:53–57)

1706 Joseph's 10 older brothers come to buy grain, but they don't recognize Joseph. Joseph accuses them of being a band of spies and of coming to engage in spying. To test their story of an aged father and a younger brother (Benjamin) at home, Joseph says that he will sell them grain, but one brother will have to remain behind as a hostage, or "earnest." When the brothers return with this so-called younger brother, Joseph promises to return the hostage to them. The brothers speak in their native tongue, unaware that Joseph can understand every word they say. Reuben says that these things are coming upon them because of what they had done to

Joseph years before. Joseph is touched by what
Reuben is saying but selects Simeon as the
hostage to stay behind. Joseph further tests the
brothers' honesty by filling their sacks with
money, which isn't discovered until the brothers return home. (Genesis 42)

1706 Jacob, who has mourned for years over
Joseph, refuses to allow Benjamin to go to
Egypt. (Genesis 42:36–38)

1705 Jacob agrees to allow the brothers to return
to Egypt with Benjamin, since the family's
grain has finally run out. Joseph tests his
brothers to determine if they've developed any
character since they sold him into slavery.
Joseph astonishes his brothers while serving
them dinner at his home. He seats the men in
correct birth order and also gives Benjamin
better food, and a five-times larger portion.
As a final test, when his brothers are ready to
leave, Joseph again has money put into the
grain sacks, and his own silver cup put into
Benjamin's sack. After the brothers leave,
Joseph sends his steward to catch up with
them, search them, and accuse them of theft.
The steward is ordered to say that Joseph's silver cup is missing, and sure enough, the evidence is discovered in Benjamin's sack. Judah
makes an eloquent plea to be punished and de-
tained instead of Benjamin. Joseph can't bear
to hide his identity any longer and finally reveals himself to his brothers in a heart-wrench-
ing scene. (Genesis 43–45)

1705 Jacob, now 130 years old, brings his family of 66 descendants, wives, servants, and employees to Egypt. They establish themselves at Goshen, in the Nile Delta. (Genesis 46–47)

1704-1700 Following Joseph's plans, starving people buy grain from Egypt, often selling everything they have. Many agree to become slaves in exchange for food. Pharaoh becomes exceedingly rich. (Genesis 47:13-19)

1700 The famine ends, and Pharaoh owns most of the land. (Genesis 47:20-26)

1689 Jacob adopts Joseph's sons, Ephraim and Manasseh, who were born to Asenath. Jacob considers them as his own; he blesses them and predicts the destiny of their descendants. (Genesis 48–49)

1688 Jacob dies in Egypt at 147 years of age. His body is eventually buried in Canaan. (Genesis 49:29–50:14)

1643 Joseph dies in Egypt at the age of 110. His body is embalmed and kept in Egypt until the Exodus. (Genesis 50:22-26)

1600-1450 The Israelites prosper in Egypt and thrive until a new king, whom Joseph didn't know, rises to power. (Exodus 1:1-8)

1450 The contributions of Joseph and the Israelites to Egypt's prosperity are eventually forgotten. Egyptian leaders arise who don't know the Israelites' history, and the Jews begin to be brutalized, forced to work at hard labor. (Exodus 1:11-14)

RIVALRY

broken brotherhood
Genesis 37:1-11

Jacob is a responsible father figure (called a patri-arch) over a large household and a thriving live-stock business. His 10 oldest sons, on the other hand, are headstrong and quarrelsome. They even inflicted revenge on a whole town because one per-son raped their sister. Yet despite their disobedi-ence, God plans for Jacob's sons to father the 12 tribes of Israel. He plans for them to be the bearers of His mission of salvation.

To mold the brothers for this role, God selects number 11 for special treatment, the adolescent Joseph, whose 10 older siblings detest him for two reasons. First, he is Jacob's favorite. Second, he dreams about his family bowing down to him as their master.

One day Joseph has a dream. When he tells it to his brothers, they hate him even more. He says to

The patriarchs

Genesis records the Life stories of ancient biblical Leaders--including Abraham, Isaac, Jacob, and Joseph--that span was more than 700 years. These individuals, known as the patriarchs, were used by God to unfold His message of salvation. The word "patriarch" is connected to the idea of fatherhood. The people, families, tribes, and nations that are represented by the patriarchs established the Line through which the Messiah (Jesus) came (see Acts 7:8; Romans 9:5; 15:8; and Hebrews 7:4).

them, "Listen to this dream I had: We were binding sheaves of grain out in the field when suddenly my sheaf rose and stood upright, while your sheaves gathered around mine and bowed down to it."

His brothers bark, "You're going to rule us? You're going to boss us around?"

Later, Joseph has yet another dream, and he shares it with his family: "The sun and the moon and 11 stars bowed down to me!"

Jacob rebukes his son: "What's with all this dreaming? Am I and your mother and your brothers all supposed to bow down to you?"

The brothers burn with jealousy and wonder more and more loudly among themselves: *What's to be done with this dreamer?*[1]

Was Joseph bragging? That's hard to say. As record-holding baseball player Babe Ruth once said, "No braggin'—just fact." You could argue that Joseph should have just kept his mouth shut, that such a dream and its interpretation were bound to inspire envy and jealousy. But, on the other hand, Joseph sincerely believed that this dream came from God. And when God gives some- one a message, it must be proclaimed, no matter how difficult it is to hear.

Be the living expression of God's kindness.
—Mother Teresa

In the first 10 verses of Genesis 37, we learn that Joseph was a confident, bold young man, much loved by his father—and envied by his brothers. Neither Joseph nor Jacob understood the depths of the brothers' hatred. That jealousy, and the strange blindness of Joseph and Jacob to it, changed the family's destiny.

What's more, this passage gives us a glimpse into family dysfunction and how God wants us to make life better on the home front.

CAN'T A GUY GET A LITTLE REVENGE?

A woman was driving down a winding road one morning when she encountered a man zooming along in the opposite direction. He veered into her lane, nearly running her off the pavement.

The man leaned out his window and hollered, "Pig!"

The woman thought she had been insulted, so she leaned out her window and yelled, "Hog!"

Joseph's dad: the world's ultimate wrestler?

The competition began in pitch dark and lasted until dawn. It was "Jacob versus God"—a match unlike any the world had ever known. God came to Jacob in a form that Jacob could wrestle with. By morning Jacob's hip was injured so that he limped, and he had a new name: Israel—"he struggles with God." The Lord said to the stubborn Hebrew, "You've wrestled with God and you've come through" (Genesis 32:28, MSG). After 20 years of resistance and a face-to-face encounter with his creator, Jacob had been broken. And even though he limped away from the encounter, he was transformed. He was now a true son of God's promise. Jacob called the place Peniel, saying, "It is because I saw God face to face, and yet my life was spared" (verse 30). (Check out Genesis 32:22-32 for the full story.)

Just then, she drove around the corner and had the shock of her life. You guessed it: She ran right into . . . *a pig!*

The moral of the story is this: Hold your temper and have the good sense to distinguish an *insult* from a *warning.*

When I feel threatened and disrespected, my natural impulse is to behave like the woman: I lash back. As we sometimes say in my home state of North Carolina: "Give as good as you get!"

Yet one of the remarkable things about Joseph is that even when he was mistreated, he maintained a humble spirit and a tender heart. He

Joseph means "increaser"

Proverbs 22:1 says, "A good name is more desirable than great riches." Joseph certainly lived up to his name. God took an act of hostility against this Hebrew and used it to preserve life—the lives of the Israelites, the Egyptians, and all the nations that came to Egypt to buy food during a severe famine. God took a life—Joseph's life—and used it to preserve his people so that one day a savior would be born to save the world.

seemed to have an ability to shine even in the most difficult of circumstances. More than any other figure in Scripture, except for Jesus Himself, Joseph was innocent of the wrongs he was accused of, and not deserving of the punishment he received.

Joseph's greatest suffering came at the hands of his own family. I firmly believe that families are God's primary way of shaping and revealing our character. There's no doubt that what we call a "dysfunctional family" today is the source of many problems in a person's life. And can you think of any family more dysfunctional than Joseph's? He had a father who showed blatant favoritism, and brothers who let rivalry go so far that they wanted to kill him.

Don't let failure go to your heart or success go to your head.

Yet Joseph never complained. (At least we don't see a hint of this in Scripture.) Instead, Joseph trusted God. He was convinced that his trials had a

Got a family feud?

As long as you focus only on your family's problems, life probably won't improve. One of the
worst things you can get from a less-than-perfect
family is a negative attitude toward life. The bottom line is this: with determination and practice,
your communication skills will improve. Remember, good communication keeps doors open, but
bad communication may end up shutting and lock-
ing the door. Here are some things I've learned
over time that help keep my family having more
fun than fury:

    1. Respect family members. If your parents or

divine purpose. He believed that good things would
one day come from bad circumstances.

    Joseph was right.

STRIVE TO BE A PEACEMAKER

Get over it! No family is perfect. The Bible makes it
clear that everybody messes up, big time: "For all
have sinned and fall short of the glory of God"
(Romans 3:23).

    Messed-up hearts, twisted values, complete
moral disorder. That's what sin is—unfaith, unlove,
unlife. It's an offense against the God of order,
beauty, and justice. All sin is detestable to God—
from telling a little white lie to committing murder
to having a rebellious attitude. Sin separates God
from humans, and that creates a problem for you

siblings tick you off, never—I repeat, never—fire
back with an angry remark. This only raises de-
fenses and widens the gap between you. A con-
trolled temper and a respectful tone allow for a
better chance at conflict resolution.

2. Focus on static-free communication. Stay
away from blanket statements. Phrases like "you
never," "you always," and "you don't ever" sound ac-
cusatory and cause the listener to become defen-
sive. Instead, stress your particular wants and
feelings by using "I." For example, "I want" or "I
feel" are effective places to begin.

and me. Even as Christians, you and I struggle with
sin, and we will for the rest of our lives on earth.
(The only sinless person is Jesus Christ: God in the
flesh.) So what's the answer? How can sinful men
and women have eternal peace with our holy God,
let alone peace in our families? Accept Christ's free
gift of forgiveness and then live a life set apart for
God to work through you.

Then, in turn, offer this forgiveness to those
who live with you. Take this test: Which label best
describes your family: (a) "the Brady Bunch,"
(b) "Jacob's Clan," or (c) "fill in the blank." Like most
people, you probably chose "c" and wrote something
like "Wonderfully Bizarre—Sort of 'The Bradys Meet
Jacob's Clan!' "

While every family has its quirks and problems,
deep down there are things you wouldn't change,

right? After all, who else kind of looks like you, knows most of your secrets (like the fact that you still sleep with that crusty teddy bear you've had since your first birthday), puts up with your annoying mood swings, and still enjoys hanging out with you? Hey, there's no place like home.

Joseph's story gives us proof that God can use even an angry family for His good. But make sure you do what you can to keep your family relationships healthy; learn from Joseph. A good dose of forgiveness can work miracles.

ADVERSITY

sweet dreams, chilling nightmares
Genesis 37:12-36

Is it another dream—or is it a *nightmare?*

Joseph's brothers are on him, whirling him around and ripping off his robe. He is struck again and again—on his side and in the small of his back. Then they drag him over dirt and rock and fling him into a cistern.

He hits the ground with a sickening *thud!* Joseph coughs and gasps for air. He looks up and sees the opening of the pit and the outlines of his brothers blocking the sunlight.

His journey through the wilderness to find his brothers turns ugly.

Will I survive? Is my life about to end? O Lord, You are with me.

When we imagine Joseph and his brothers tending sheep, we might think of them in a nearby pasture

Twelve sons, twelve tribes

The 12 tribes, descended from Jacob's 12 sons, occupied the Promised Land. But eventually 10 tribes were rejected because of their faithlessness, leaving only the southern kingdom of Judah. Then Judah's inhabitants were taken into exile, and attention focused on the "remnant," which would later return to the land. Finally, just one man, Jesus Christ, came on the scene, the one in whom God's will would be perfectly fulfilled. Jesus is also known as "the Lion of the tribe of Judah" (Revelation 5:5).

or on a hillside above their village. But in the semi-arid country of what today is modern-day Israel, sheepherders roamed for many miles in search of grass and water. It doesn't seem like a big deal when we read in verse 12 that the brothers were grazing Jacob's flocks near Shechem. But pull out a map, and you'll discover that this town is 50 miles north of Hebron, where Jacob's headquarters were located.

The situation came to a head when Jacob said to Joseph, "Go and see if all is well with your brothers and with the flocks, and bring word back to me" (Genesis 37:14).

So Joseph made the long, dangerous trek to Shechem. The land he hiked was inhabited by murderous Canaanites and Perizzites (see Genesis 34:30). But when Joseph arrived in Shechem, after a journey that may have taken several days, he was

Hebrew herdsmen

Joseph grew up in a family of hardworking herds-
men. His father and brothers spent long hours
tending to cattle in a rugged land called Canaan.
(FYI: The word "cattle" in the Bible has a broader
meaning of "livestock"—cows and goats, as well as
sheep, mules, horses, and even camels.) His family's hard work paid off. According to Genesis 30:43,
Jacob's thriving livestock business made him a
wealthy man: "The man got richer and richer, acquiring huge flocks, lots and lots of servants, not
to mention camels and donkeys" (MSG).

told that his brothers had gone farther north still,
to Dothan, a town situated along the trade routes
to Egypt. We can only speculate why Joseph's brothers might have wandered so far from their Hebron
Valley home. Perhaps the weather had been particu-
larly dry that year, and the movement was necessary to keep from overgrazing any one region. Or
perhaps it was simply because Jacob's flocks were
so vast that they required a huge range.

Indeed, Jacob was a shrewd businessman who
sought power and wealth—perhaps too much at
times.

Or it could be that roaming so far from home
was part of the brothers' plan all along. But that
seems unlikely, since we learn in verses 17 and 18
that "Joseph went after his brothers and found
them near Dothan. But they saw him in the dis-
tance, and before he reached them, they plotted to

What's so special about a robe?

It was an extravagant gift for a boy of Joseph's age: a richly ornamented robe. Not only did it set apart the teen as his father's favorite, but it gave Joseph the appearance of royalty in his own household. That fact alone added insult to injury in the eyes of his jealous older brothers. To fully grasp the significance of Jacob's gift to Joseph, let's take a crash course in ancient clothing customs:

Hebrew men often wore a protective outer garment (me'yil) that they referred to as a coat, robe, or mantle. It was wrapped tightly around their bodies and drawn in close by a belt (or girdle).

Robes of the poor were made of coarsely

kill him." This Scripture seems to imply that their grudge against Joseph was long-standing, but the plot to kill him came to them suddenly.

Dothan, the nearby town, was so named because the word means "two cis-terns." There were two huge, well-known storage wells there, one of which had gone dry by Joseph's time. So one of the broth-ers, Reuben, talked his brothers into throwing Joseph down into the cistern rather than killing him. Then Judah, after Reuben left for a while, saw a caravan of Ishmaelites bound for Egypt passing nearby and sug-

Feeling down? Remember: God is in control. "Be still, and know that I am God." (Psalm 46:10)

woven goat's hair and served as bed clothing. (see
Exodus 22:26-27.)

The rich viewed their robes as symbols of
honor, status, and power. Wealthy men wore gar-
ments made of fine linens and imported silk.
Many were embroidered with gold threads and
elaborate patterns.

A man being installed in a position of honor or
importance was given a special robe. For example,
Joseph was given such a robe in Egypt when he was
put in a leadership position. (see Genesis 41:42.)

Taking away a robe signaled a man's removal
from high position.

According to Luke 15:22, a fine robe was a mark
of a man's honor in his household.

gested selling Joseph to this group. They did so, for
20 shekels of silver, thereby getting rid of their
problem but cleverly keeping themselves free of
blood guilt. Instead they fabricated their brother's
death (see Genesis 37:26-35).

THE TEST

Many years ago a guy named Jonathan Blanchard
bought a used book. He noticed handwritten notes
in the margins and began to enjoy the previous
owner's thoughts nearly as much as the book itself.
Blanchard discovered that the book had belonged
to a woman named Miss Hollis Mayfield.

Blanchard was in Ohio; Mayfield was in New York.

On a whim he wrote to her, and to his amazement, he got a response. The two began to correspond.

Eventually Blanchard felt that he was falling in love with Miss Mayfield, even though they had never met in person. By mutual agreement it was decided that Blanchard would travel to New York and that the two would meet in the terminal at Grand Central Station.

"Send me a photo of yourself," Blanchard requested.

"No," said the woman. "If this is truly love, does it matter how I look?"

Blanchard asked how he would recognize her. She explained that she would have on a green outfit and would wear a red rose in the lapel of her jacket.

Once at the huge New York station, Blanchard scanned the crowd. His eyes searched wildly for the woman he thought he loved and whom he hoped would love him in return. At one point he noticed a beautiful woman standing by a wall, in a green outfit. But, with disappointment, he noticed that she didn't have a red rose in her lapel.

Eventually an older, stooped woman began to approach Blanchard. She was quite unattractive, but she wore green and had a red rose in her lapel. The man felt a choke of disappointment in his throat. Blanchard's hopes and expectations were apparently shattered.

For a brief moment he thought of walking out.

Satan is the Enemy

"Be self-controlled and alert. Your enemy the devil prowls around like a roaring lion looking for someone to devour" (1 Peter 5:8).

Don't be fooled; Satan exists. The Bible uses various names to describe him—Lucifer, Beelzebub, the Devil, the serpent, the Dragon, the fallen angel, the Enemy—and scripture makes it clear that he is evil. Satan and his troops are viciously attacking the kingdom of God. His target: our souls. So, how can you survive? Have a personal, active relationship with Jesus Christ. The Lord is your ultimate ally, your ultimate Defender.

He reasoned that the woman had never seen him, and not knowing what he looked like, it might be possible for him to slip away, unnoticed. He could discreetly leave, as if the planned meeting had never happened.

But his character and integrity wouldn't allow it. Blanchard straightened himself, forced a smile, and approached the woman with the rose in her lapel. He extended his hand. "Ma'am," he began, "I am Jonathan Blanchard." With a big smile he said, "It would be my great honor to take you to dinner."

They made conversation for a brief moment. Then the woman looked up to him and said, "Young man, I don't know what this is all about. But I was asked to wear this red rose in my lapel and was told that if you offered to take me to dinner, we would be joined by that beautiful young lady over there."

Miss Mayfield, the beautiful young lady in the

green outfit whom Jonathan had seen earlier, now knew that Jonathan Blanchard was genuine, sincere ... *authentic.*

God tests us, too. It's not a game for Him. And He certainly isn't toying with our emotions. More often, the Lord is preparing us for the dreams in our own hearts.

As you read Joseph's story, compare the boy at the beginning to the older, wiser man at the end. The young Joseph had no regard for his brothers' feelings. Joseph's dreams and the way he described them alienated his brothers. Yet as he matured, Joseph's heart broke with love and affection for his brothers—despite the fact that they had wronged him, giving him more reason for anger, bitterness, and revenge.

> *Jesus [said], "What is impossible with men is possible with God." (Luke 18:27)*

Adversity put Joseph through the refiner's fire, and he emerged a much purer man. God transformed him into an overcomer who not only loved his own family but who would be used to save an entire nation.

TURN TO GOD DURING TIMES OF TROUBLE

Adversity doesn't mean disaster. Consider the trials of some of history's most famous overcomers:

- Demosthenes, greatest orator of the ancient world, stuttered. The first time he tried to make a public speech, he was laughed off the platform.

- Julius Caesar was an epileptic.
- Beethoven began losing his hearing in his 20s and eventually became completely deaf.
- Thomas Edison, who was hard of hearing, tried and failed so many times at inventing the lightbulb, lab assistants began to mock him.
- John Bunyan spent 12 years of his adult life in a prison cell, but he gave Christendom a book called *Pilgrim's Progress*, which has been in print since 1678.
- Glenn Cunningham, before setting the world's record for running the mile, was once burned so severely that doctors told him he would never walk again.

God worked in Joseph's life, and He has been at work in the lives of other overcomers throughout history. Sometimes the only way God can bless us is by breaking us. It's not easy, and it's not fun. We feel alone, wrestling and questioning, feeling empty and full of doubts—not aware that we might, in fact, be very close to an amazing encounter with God.

At times that's how God gets our attention. It's how God worked in Joseph's life. When everything was going great, perhaps the young man couldn't hear Him very well. Yet when Joseph found himself wandering through a spiritual desert—when he struggled—God had Joseph's undivided attention. Twentieth-century scholar and author C. S. Lewis put it this way: "God whispers to us in our pleasures . . . but shouts in our pains."[1]

Could you be on the verge of some incredible new

stage of spiritual growth in your life? Are you determined to be counted among God's overcomers?

Consider this insight from nineteenth-century
Bible scholar Charles Spurgeon:

> When the light comes the darkness must de-
> part. Where truth is, the lie must flee. If the
> lie remains, there will be a severe conflict, be-
> cause truth cannot and will not lower its stan-
> dard. If you follow Christ, all the hounds of the
> world will yelp at your heels.[2]

Living on the side of truth means adversity:
saying *no* when all your friends are saying *yes*, or
yes when they're saying *no*; holding back anger
when you want to lash out; being honest when you
know that a little bit of dishonesty could make life
easier.

When it feels as if the Christian life involves
more pain and problems than blessing and bliss,
consider this: It's better to endure temporary struggle, which leads to eternal joy, than momentary
comfort, which results in everlasting torment. Keep
in mind the following truths about suffering:

1. Suffering never gets as nasty as hell. Whether
your pain is short term or long term, it *will* end.
Even if your suffering lasts all your earthly life,
heaven's welcome mat will read "no tears." But hell
is agony (see Luke 16:24).

2. Suffering cannot be avoided. Living in a
messed-up, sinful world involves pain (see John

16:33). Your only choice is deciding if you'll become bitter about it or turn to God for help to find joy despite the pain (James 1:2-4).

3. Suffering brings Jesus close. In your every struggle, Jesus suffers with you (see 2 Corinthians 1:5).

Here's how popular author Henry Blackaby explains it:

> God will not necessarily take your problems away, but He will carry the load for you. He wants you to experience His peace, which is beyond human comprehension. You will never fully understand how God could give you peace in some of the situations you face, but you do not have to understand it in order to experience it.... Scripture says to be anxious for nothing. God's Word clearly indicates that there is nothing you can face that is too difficult, too troubling, or too fearful for God.[3]

ATTITUDE

the favored slave
Genesis 39:1-6

Joseph is alive! He survives his brothers' beating and lives to see another day. But now he faces another unthinkable challenge: He has been sold to slave traders and is standing on an auction platform in Egypt.

Will I face more struggle? Will I ever return home? O Lord, I know You are with me.

A powerful man named Potiphar, one of Pharaoh's officials and the captain of the guard, buys the boy and takes him to his house: a palatial estate of marble-white walls, interior courtyards, fountains, and latticed windows.

In the days that follow, life gets better for Joseph. God is with him, and things begin to look up. Even Potiphar recognizes that the Lord is with the boy and sees that God is working for good in everything he does. He becomes fond of Joseph and makes him his personal aide.

From that moment on, God blesses the home of the Egyptian—all because of Joseph. The blessing of God spreads over everything he owns, at home and in the fields.[1]

Remember, the Ishmaelites—also called the Midianites—continued on their trade journey to Egypt. When they arrived there, they sold Joseph to Potiphar, a very powerful man described as "the captain of the guard" (Genesis 39:1). This is a telling detail. Had Joseph been an average man, they would likely have sold him as a laborer or a tradesman. But even the Ishmaelites were able to identify that Joseph was a young man of significant gifts.

Again, even in slavery "the LORD was with Joseph and he prospered" (verse 2). As Joseph demonstrated, it's all about attitude. You can strive to be a winner if you maintain a positive mind-set and a heart that's faithful to God, regardless of your circumstances.

> *People who inspire others are those who see invisible bridges at the end of dead-end streets.*
> —Charles Swindoll, Dropping Your Guard

Turn to the book of Judges for snapshot after snapshot of raw, uncensored *failure*: "Then the Israelites did evil in the eyes of the LORD and served the Baals" (Judges 2:11). Keep reading, and you'll discover that despite humankind's gross unfaithfulness, *God is faithful.* He

Egypt's middle-kingdom period

The year: 1876 B.C. The place: Egypt during the middle-kingdom period. Young Joseph was snatched from his boyhood home in the rolling hills of Canaan and dropped off in a mysterious land of pyramids and pharaohs. Little did he realize he'd one day be a big success in this strange place, rising from servant to vizier (second in power to the ruler). It was an exciting time to be in Egypt. The kingdom was trading commercial goods with Crete, Palestine, Syria, and other lands. Art and literature blossomed, and peaceful conditions prevailed. When Jacob and his family caught up with Joseph in Egypt, they no doubt felt secure from attack and persecution.

molds and disciplines His children. He shows persistent, unwearied love and matchless grace—grace that's absolutely underserved. Time and again, God demonstrates His gracious divine deliverance. When Israel was attacked, "Then the LORD raised up judges, who saved [the Israelites] out of the hands of these raiders" (verse 16).

"GOD, WILL YOU PLEASE MAKE THE IMPOSSIBLE POSSIBLE?"

I've asked this question more than once throughout my life. And each time I've discovered the same thing: God always provides, and He always knows best.

Proverbs principles

As the old saying goes, "when life gives you lemons, make lemonade!" That's exactly what Joseph did as he stayed close to God and turned hardship into happiness. Perhaps he drew from the timeless success principles found in the book of Proverbs:

- Proverbs principle: "[wisdom] will save you also from the adulteress, from the wayward wife with her seductive words, who has left the partner of her youth and ignored the covenant she made before God. For her house leads down to death and her paths to the spirits of the dead. None who go to her return or attain the paths of life" (Proverbs 2:16-19).

Sometimes we have to wait for God's plan to become visible to us, and that can be challenging. But history is full of the stories of many godly people who experienced God's faithfulness and timely intervention firsthand.

Back in 1990 a group of Christians decided to build a camp high in Colorado's Rocky Mountains. Shortly after acquiring the land, the leaders realized they didn't have enough money to excavate and build a road to their facility. But instead of becoming discouraged, the leaders maintained positive attitudes, put their trust in God, and sought His guidance through prayer. Weeks passed, and no answer seemed immediately clear. Without sufficient funds, the group's desire for a way through the wilderness would simply have to wait.

- Joseph's choice: He resisted sexual temptation and stayed faithful to God. (see Genesis 39:7-12.)
- Proverbs principle: "The fear of the LORD is the beginning of knowledge, but fools despise wisdom and discipline" (Proverbs 1:7).
- Joseph's choice: He attributed his success to reverence for God. (see Genesis 42:18.)
- Proverbs principle: "Many are the plans in a man's heart, but it is the LORD's purpose that prevails" (Proverbs19:21).
- Joseph's choice: He knew that God's will overrules human plans. (see Genesis 45:5-8.)

But their prayers for a road were answered in an unusual way.

A marble company that was moving equipment nearby had lost a valuable crane. (The machine had tumbled down the mountain, landing in a valley.) Workers needed to create a road across the mountain to retrieve the crane. But to reach it, the company would need to cross over land owned by the camp.

"Would it be okay if we built a road—at our expense, of course—down the mountain and into the valley?" asked a company representative.

It wasn't hard for the camp leaders to give their blessing!

There can be no doubt that an unwavering trust in God and His sovereignty goes a long way toward helping us maintain a positive attitude when hard times hit. When life gets weird and our trials seem bigger than a mountain in the Rockies, the knowledge that God allows challenges for a reason is a comfort. And when things are going well for us, experiencing those blessings is a great joy as well.

We can fix our eyes on our circumstances or cling to God and choose to worship Him, even when it hurts.
–Matt Redman,
The Unquenchable Worshipper

Having the right attitude makes a difference!

MAKE AN ATTITUDE CHANGE

Twentieth-century pastor and author A. W. Tozer wrote, "No man is worthy to succeed until he is willing to fail."

Tozer explained it this way: "God may allow His servant to succeed when He has disciplined him to a point where he does not need to succeed to be happy. The man who is elated by success and cast down by failure is still a carnal man. At best his fruit will have a worm in it."[2]

In God's perfect time, He gives a new beginning to people who so easily turn their backs on Him; rebellious children who break promises; generations that know more than a little about failure—people like you and me.

When life is tough, and you feel like a failure, remember the following:

1. It's a bigger mistake to turn your back on God when life gets hard. He's always there; reach out to Him. Not only will He comfort and protect you from the humiliation the world dishes out when you fail, but He'll also actually turn your sorrow into joy.

2. Don't be paralyzed by hardships. The Lord wants to transform tremendously flawed individuals into heroes who are fit to accomplish His purposes. Don't let life's struggles defeat you. Instead, *let God have His way.*

3. Consider Saint Augustine's prayer for freedom:

Almighty God, in whom we live and move and have our being, who hast made us for thyself, so that our hearts are restless till they rest in thee: Grant us purity of heart and strength of purpose, that no selfish passion may hinder us from knowing thy will, no weakness from doing it; but that in thy light we may see light clearly, and in thy service find perfect freedom; through Jesus Christ our Lord.[3]

GOD'S TRUTH SETS US FREE

Too often, contemporary Christian culture is a result of following trends, not following Christ. Yet being a Christian isn't about wearing a certain shirt, reading a certain magazine, or even going to church every Sunday. Being a Christian means that you (1) agree that Jesus Christ is Lord and Savior (Romans 10:9-10), (2) repent of your sins and ask

Him to forgive your sins (Acts 3:19; 13:38), and (3) take up your cross daily and follow Jesus (Luke 9:23-24). Being a Christian means living by the absolute, timeless, eternal truth of Jesus Christ, not mirroring the passing fads of people. If you truly study and seek absolute truth, you'll find it—and God will open your eyes and transform your life. Even the apostle Paul needed vision therapy. Acts 9 tells us that after his encounter with Jesus on the road to Damascus, Paul became blind (verses 8-9). But when God sent a disciple named Ananias to heal him, "something like scales fell from [Paul's] eyes, and he could see again" (verse 18).

By studying the life of Joseph, you'll learn more about biblical role-models, God, and yourself. You'll be able to adjust your attitude easily much like you would adjust your prescription for glasses or contact lenses.

OBEDIENCE

fighting temptations
Genesis 39:7-19

Joseph is well-built and handsome, and after a while his master's wife becomes infatuated with him. One day she whispers a shocking invitation into Joseph's ear, words he can hardly believe: "Come to bed with me!"

"Look, with me here," the young Hebrew tells her, "my master doesn't give a second thought to anything that goes on here—he's put me in charge of everything he owns. He treats me as an equal. The only thing he hasn't turned over to me is you. You're his wife, after all! How could I violate his trust and sin against God?"

She pesters him day after day, but Joseph doesn't give in. He refuses to sleep with her—or even to be in the same room with her.

One day Joseph comes to the house to work, and the woman becomes so aggressive that he has no choice but to flee. Joseph leaves his cloak in her hands as he wrenches himself from her grasp. When Potiphar's wife realizes that she has his coat, she calls to her servants: "Look . . . this Hebrew has been brought to us to make sport of us! He came in here to sleep with me, but I screamed. When he heard me scream for help, he left his cloak beside me and ran out of the house."

She keeps Joseph's coat beside her until his master comes home. Then she repeats the same story, telling her husband, "That Hebrew slave you brought us came to me to make sport of me."

When Potiphar hears the story, he burns with anger.[1]

In modern times Potiphar's wife would have been right at home with the TV characters on *Desperate Housewives*. She was rich, bored, and didn't have a relationship with God to curb her wickedness. She tried repeatedly to seduce Joseph, and the young man steadfastly resisted. But it was tough for him. This woman was brazen and insistent. Scripture is more direct on this point than is often the case: "Come to bed with me!" she said. It doesn't get much more direct than that.

Joseph's refusal put him in a precarious situation. He was a slave whose life depended upon keeping his powerful master happy, so he couldn't simply run away. On the other hand, in the class-conscious Egyptian culture, neither could he reveal what

Potiphar's wife was doing. She would either deny it or possibly even argue that sexual favors were her right as the mistress of the household—just like the wealthy men who sometimes claimed this right.

Another dimension to this story is often overlooked. It's possible, even likely, that Potiphar was a eunuch. Often, in pagan cultures, men who rose from lower classes to positions of authority were considered threats to the royal families. These men had to submit to being castrated to keep their positions of authority and enjoy the luxuries that went with them. If they refused, they were stripped of their office and sent back to the lower classes. It was a horrible choice for both the man and his wife, but one that men often made so they could experience the privileges of wealth in an age when comfort wasn't easily found.

Of course, this doesn't excuse the behavior of Potiphar's wife. I want to make that point because we often read stories in Scripture and think, *Well, things are so much different today. Right and wrong, good and evil—it's so much more complicated to know what the right answer is.* But situations are complicated in every age. Regardless of how tough life can get, God requires one thing of us: obedience.

That's exactly how Joseph reacted: He obeyed God and His principles. Joseph avoided Potiphar's wife the best way he knew how. In an important household like Potiphar's, there were often many servants around. We can also assume that the

Standing strong (when it's easier to give in)

Doing what's right comes with a price. But as Joseph discovered, the cost of following God is worth every sacrifice we must make. So when the pressure hits, what are the keys to standing strong? Actually, it involves some faith training long before we face a tough choice. Start today by taking two faith steps.

Faith step No. 1: Identify hypocrisy in your own life. Hey, it's not hard to miss. You say one thing, then you act another way; you make promises, then you break them; you find faults in others but

house was large, with two or three floors. Joseph probably worked on the first floor, while the family he served spent most of their time on the upper levels. Perhaps Joseph's strategy for avoiding Potiphar's wife was to stay busy on the bottom floor and not venture upstairs unless other servants were around. But one day, for reasons we don't know, all the servants left the house. That's when Potiphar's wife made her moves.

We have no record of Joseph defending himself against the woman's false accusations. Perhaps he did, but his defense failed to convince Potiphar. Or maybe he felt that any defense would be pointless. One possibility is that he purposefully remained silent to avoid shaming Potiphar, who, after all, had treated him well and was in a delicate situation himself.

overlook your own; you call yourself a christian but catch yourself acting like the world.

Faith step no. 2: Ask Jesus to help you break free from a phony faith. Ask Him to reveal areas of your life that need work (sins to confess, habits to overcome, desires to commit to Him). Ask Him to purge the old ways of thinking and acting–especially a lifestyle filled with envy, pride, anger, jealousy, and lust. Ask Him to help you correct any wrong thinking you may have or take away any doubts that may haunt you.

In any case, Joseph once again faced unfair treatment as the all-too-familiar pattern of favor, adversity, obedience, and blessing continued to play out in the young man's life. But was this the final straw for Joseph? Would this new faith test break him?

The little things you do every day tell whether you live for yourself or for God.
—Tricia Brock of Superchic

GOD FIGHTS THE BATTLE FOR YOU

Put yourself in Joseph's sandals. If someone constantly tempted you to have sex, how would you have reacted? (Be honest with yourself.) My prayer is that you, too, would have stood strong in obedience to God. But consider this: Even if you're a

What does integrity look like?

Joseph knew that without integrity, he wouldn't have much of a future. Proverbs 10:9 says, "[A person] of integrity walks securely." That's what you want, isn't it? If your desire is to walk through life with confidence, to walk like Joseph, then you need integrity.

- Integrity serves as a guide for life's moral decisions. (Proverbs 11:3)
- A person of integrity hates falsehood in every form. (Proverbs 13:5-6)
- Integrity is something to be held on to, even in tough times. (Job 2:3)
- A person of integrity keeps his word, even when it hurts to do so. (Psalm 15:1-4)

Christian, your old nature still exists. And if you give it a chance by encouraging it, it literally takes control. The result is a strained relationship with God. So, how can you make things right again? How can you keep your old nature from ruining your new life in Christ?

1. Confession is the healing answer to a crippled walk. Jesus Christ is reaching out to you with open arms; go to Him in prayer. Tell Him all about your sins, tell Him you're sorry, and He'll forgive you— "If we confess our sins, he is faithful and just and will forgive us our sins and purify us from all unrighteousness" (1 John 1:9).

2. Repent. Once you've confessed the sin and asked Jesus to help you change (this is called *repentance*), you can trust that you're totally for-

- A person of integrity isn't afraid to run
  when temptation comes knocking.
  (2 Timothy 2:22)
- A person of integrity says both yes and no,
  when each is appropriate, and means what
  she says. (James 5:12)
- A person of integrity backs up what he
  says with how he lives. (Titus 2:7-8)
- A person of integrity understands that
  all of life is on display before God.
  (1 Kings 9:4)
- Integrity is what God looks for in a person's character. (1 Chronicles 29:17)

given. Now, with your relationship fully restored
with God, you can take steps toward growth and
change. (The Holy Spirit will help you.)

3. *Live with eternity in mind.* The whole issue of
dying is probably the furthest thing from your
mind. But stop for a moment and ask yourself a few
questions: If I died tomorrow, would I go to heaven?
Is death the end? How will I deal with the inevitable
loss of those I love so much? Will they have eternal
life? Death stings. It's an enemy—of both God and
humans—not a friend. But if you're a Christian, you
know that your final heartbeat won't be the mysterious end to life. And you know that when you stand
at the graveside of a Christian brother or sister,
your loss is only temporary. That date when you
and other believers meet Jesus face-to-face will be

the ultimate homecoming. It will be the grand beginning to a life that never ends. The apostle Paul
wrote, "The sting of death is sin, and the power of
sin is the law. But thanks be to God! He gives us the
victory through our Lord Jesus Christ" (1 Corinthians 15:56-57).

BIG-LEAGUE OBEDIENCE

Joseph stood strong and was obedient to God,
even when it cost him everything. Let me tell you
about another young man who wouldn't compromise his values.

By age 17 Kent Bottenfield was slated to become
the next big thing in Major League Baseball. And
by his mid-20s Ken was living his dream. He played
for such teams as the Colorado Rockies, the San
Francisco Giants, and the St. Louis Cardinals. In
1999 he was a starting pitcher in the All-Star Game,
throwing pitches at Roger Clemens and striking
out the famed Derek Jeter.

But as a Christian in the fast-paced world of professional sports, life wasn't always easy for Kent.
Although he got to play the sport he'd loved since
childhood—and got paid for it!—he constantly had
to fight the temptations that came with life on the
road. Kent was often teased for not looking at
pornography while riding on the bus. And he was
repulsed when he learned that some of his team-
mates often hired spies—lookouts who made sure
that their wives wouldn't catch them cheating.

Every day Kent had to endure taunts and name-calling: "How's our Altar Boy today? Is he still too holy to hang with the guys?"

The young athlete didn't walk the narrow path of righteousness because he thought it would make him popular. He followed the Lord because he knew it was *right.* His life verse was Romans 14:8: "If we live, we live to the Lord; and if we die, we die to the Lord. So, whether we live or die, we belong to the Lord."

Kent made his mark in the Major Leagues. He often appeared in *USA Today* and on ESPN, and after the famous Dave Dravecky left the San Francisco Giants, Kent was the first player to wear his number. It would be natural to assume that baseball was Kent's *life.* Yet this athlete's number-one priority was his relationship with Jesus Christ.

His spiritual maturity would be tested and proven in the last couple of years he played professional sports. During batting practice one day, a ball from a pitching machine accidentally hit him. The device hurled the ball at nearly 100 miles per hour, and the impact resulted in the first of several shoulder injuries that would ultimately end Kent's career.

But Kent wasn't angry with the person in charge of the machine; he forgave the staff member and put his situation in God's hands. He played on and played well; however, recurrent bouts of pain became increasingly intense. After performing exploratory surgery, doctors told Kent that his shoulder muscles were going to deteriorate further and that he could pitch only one more season.

Then Kent did something that few sports figures are able to do with ease: He walked away from baseball. He chose not to put his team (or his body) through an agonizing, less-than-ideal final year, reflecting on the fact that he belonged to Christ.

Whenever temptation and "brain graffiti" mess with your mind, tell yourself this: "I am loved by God. I can do all things through Him."

When they heard about his retirement, his friends argued, "But baseball is you; baseball is your life!"

"No," Kent said. "Baseball is something I do. And, yes, I do enjoy it. But it's not my whole life. *Jesus Christ is my life.* I can lose the ability to pitch, but I can never lose Jesus."[2]

TAKE SOME GUTSY OBEDIENT STEPS

Kent Bottenfield had a lot in common with Joseph. Both men often stood alone, yet they did so confidently and unwaveringly because of their righteousness. You'd be wise to stand strong when the going gets tough. Here's how:

1. *Ask God to help you be* obedient *to Him in every area of your life.* Although the cost of obedience is expensive, the reward is unreal: "This is the confidence we have in approaching God: that if we ask anything according to his will, he hears

us. And if we know that he hears us—whatever we ask—we know that we have what we asked of him" (1 John 5:14-15).

2. Remove the roadblocks. Let Jesus search your heart and pinpoint specific sins that are holding you back from an obedient relationship with Him. After praying, take out a notebook and a pen. On the top left-hand side of one page, write "Things I Must Get Right with God." Then list all the stuff you need to confess to the Lord. Ask God to do a deep work in your soul. Allow Him to examine every area of your life. (Example: Perhaps you have a problem with envy or a bad temper. Confess these sins to God.)

3. Run from temptation. Even though running caused Joseph to end up in prison, he was willing to trust God for the consequences. He knew that if he did the right thing, God would eventually vindicate him, even though his vindication seemed impossible.

4. Understand that sin is serious to God. Joseph did not bow to his own lust, or to the strategies of Potiphar's wife, or to the cultural norms of that day. It's interesting that in resisting, Joseph said, "How then could I do such a wicked thing and sin against God?" (Genesis 39:9). Joseph cared about honoring his master, Potiphar, but he also understood that the true sin would be against God—and God was sovereign. There would be an inevitable day of judgment when he would give an account of his actions to God. Joseph knew that the measure of sin isn't just in its effect upon our neighbor but in its affront to the majesty and holiness of our sovereign God.

5. Recognize that a pure mind isn't a mind free of temptation. A pure mind chooses to act in the right way when temptation strikes. Or, put another way, temptation is inevitable; what counts is how you meet it.

6. Believe what Joseph knew: God won't give up on you. In the Lord you'll find acceptance, love, and freedom—despite your shortcomings. Ask Him to go deep into your heart and heal the *real* cause of what keeps you from being obedient.

7. Accept that living for Christ is expensive—it costs everything! Especially stuff like trust, commitment, and obedience to Jesus. Here's how scholar Dietrich Bonhoeffer explained it:

> Costly grace is the gospel which must be sought again and again, the gift that must be asked for, the door at which a man must knock.
>
> Such grace is costly because it calls us to follow, and it is grace because it calls us to follow Jesus Christ. It is costly because it costs a man his life, and it is grace because it gives a man the only true life. It is costly because it condemns sin, and grace because it justifies the sinner. Above all, it is costly because it cost God the life of his Son: "ye were bought at a price," and what has cost God much cannot be cheap for us. Above all, it is grace because God did not reckon his Son too dear a price to pay for our life, but delivered him up for us. Costly grace is the Incarnation of God.[3]

TRUST

Joseph is trapped in yet another dismal hole—a basement prison. Again he's been stripped of his robe, along with the favor and responsibilities he'd enjoyed in the shadow of the powerful.

And once again Joseph faces more betrayal . . . *more heartache.*

As Joseph's eyes adjust to the darkness, he inspects his new surroundings. The walls are thick, the rooms are narrow and dark and mostly bare.

Eventually Joseph discovers many such cells, a labyrinth of rooms inhabited by men of every rank. A hidden community of unfortunate men must endure desperate conditions in this Egyptian prison. And not one man knows when he might be released since there are no fixed sentences, only the whim of the powerful people upstairs.

But right there in jail, Joseph clings to hope. *God is with him.*

The Lord reaches out in kindness to Joseph, granting him favor in the eyes of the warden. And in the days and weeks ahead, the head jailer puts Joseph in charge of all the prisoners, and he's given the responsibility of managing the whole operation.

The warden pays no attention to anything under Joseph's care; the Lord is with Joseph and gives him success in whatever he does.[1]

In Joseph's day, jails were truly grim places. The conditions were often horrible. It was common for prisoners to be denied food or to be fed sporadically and poorly. And often, people were imprisoned without any semblance of what we call the due process of law. In other words, a powerful man like Potiphar, captain of Pharaoh's guard, could simply declare Joseph guilty and send him to jail indefinitely.

Such prisoners would depend upon family members to keep them alive with food and other necessities. And often, family members would plead the prisoner's case with officials or, as often happened, would bribe those officials to release their loved one.

Joseph had no family in Egypt. He had none of those advantages. He was a stranger in a strange land, with no possibility of redemption by his kinsmen. If anyone deserved to be in despair, it was Joseph.

It's all about truth, not feelings

Faith isn't something we base on feelings. Our faith is based on the bedrock fact that God came to earth in the person of Jesus, he died for our sins, he rose again from the dead, and even today, he reigns as Lord over all. Nothing can change the truth. Not feelings, not indigestion, not cloudy days, not lousy days in school, not an argument with your parents.

Yet the young man didn't lose hope, even in prison. The Westminster Catechism—a list of questions and answers on the basics of the faith—gives us a clue about Joseph's hope: "What is the chief end of man? The chief end of man is to glorify God and enjoy Him forever."

Pray about your anxious attitude: "Lord God, I want peace, not worry. I want joy, not jitters."

Joseph never lost sight of this primary goal, this "chief end." Regardless of his situation, Joseph worshipped God, acknowledged God, and gave glory (credit) to God for anything good that happened to him. That trusting attitude served him well, despite his circumstances.

SURVIVAL TIPS WHEN LIFE DOESN'T MAKE SENSE

When you're confused about what's happening in your life, the following survival tips will help you keep a godly perspective and hold on to your hope in Jesus:

1. Remind yourself that things will get better. Your feelings rise and fall like a wild ride on a roller coaster. When everything seems to be going wrong, and life doesn't seem to be worth living, you need to ride things out. It may not feel good for a while, but if you ride out these emotions, you'll discover that your circumstances will soon change. Your world will seem much better. Happiness will return.

2. Allow yourself to cry. Don't be embarrassed by all those raw, uncomfortable feelings tangled up inside of you. Go ahead, turn your eyes toward heaven and let the tears flow. Jesus understands. He'll be right there with you.

3. Scoot in a little closer to God. Take a look at what C. S. Lewis wrote in one of his letters: "The thing is to rely only on God. The time will come when you will regard all this misery as a small price to pay for having been brought to that dependence."[2]

A TEST OF MY FAITH, PART 1

Most of our greatest triumphs grow out of struggles we encounter. Even as Christians our lives will be full of valleys *and* mountaintops. God doesn't promise a way around them but *through* them. And once we go through the valleys and over the mountains in our lives, we always come out stronger than before. The apostle Paul reminds us that "we are hard pressed on every side, but not crushed; perplexed, but not in despair; persecuted, but

God, are You listening?

God may seem far away at times. Sometimes we feel as if we talk and talk, yet we wonder if He hears us. The answer is . . . yes! God hears all of our prayers. Even when He seems silent, keep talking to Him. The book of James says that we don't have because we don't ask (4:2) and that the "prayer of a righteous man is powerful and effective" (5:16).

Again and again the Holy Scriptures reveal to us that prayer is an effective tool.

not abandoned; struck down, but not destroyed" (2 Corinthians 4:8-9).

When I lived in Greensboro, North Carolina, I dreamed of hosting an apologetics conference and had my sights set on a 5,000-seat coliseum, a place that would be neutral turf for non-Christians. I decided to call the conference "Truth for a New Generation" and invite people who had never set foot in a church.

An apologetics conference of this size and scope was a totally new concept for Christians in my hometown, as well as for believers in most other American cities. The speakers would cover deep theological content that many youth workers felt was too intense for teens.

To reserve the facility, I also had to come up with a cash deposit a year in advance, which wasn't cheap. (I determined that it would cost more than $85,000 to pull off the event.) So I withdrew my savings account and committed myself to my dream.

Soon, a year of planning, budgeting, advertising,

and promotion began. My team and I would need to sell every ticket possible to make our budget.

With less than six weeks to go, I received a call from Mr. Doug Moradian, assistant manager of the coliseum. He asked me how many tickets we had sold.

"About 400," I said with a lump in my throat.

He paused for what seemed like an eternity and then responded, "I've been in the event business many years. In my experience, the best you can do in your final weeks is to double the tickets you've sold at the one-month mark."

I did the math. Our event would probably have somewhere around 800 attendees. That wouldn't look good in a stadium with 5,000 seats! Then Mr. Moradian said, "Kid, I don't want to see you get hurt on this event. How about downsizing your event? I have a smaller auditorium that seats exactly 800 people. Your conference will look full, and if you go with the smaller facility, your costs will be reduced by about $15,000."

Mr. Moradian explained the advantages of having a smaller stage, a smaller PA system, fewer stage lights, and less technical support. I had to get back to him with an answer ASAP.

I was concerned about the slow ticket sales. And as conference bills mounted, I wondered how we could possibly cover them all. Yet in the back of my mind, it seemed as if I could hear the Lord whispering, "Alex, trust Me!"

Two weeks before the conference, we had sold

750 registrations. We were better off than we had been, but we were still a long way from 5,000. Mr. Moradian called again to see if I wanted to move down to the smaller auditorium.

"At this point you'll have to stick with whatever decision you make," he told me.

I desperately wanted to fulfill what I felt God had led me to do. But deep inside I felt afraid. I'd lie awake at night, my mind full of questions: "Did I really hear God correctly a year ago? What if these famous speakers come and preach to a room that's 90 percent empty? How will I pay back the conference bills and expenses?"

But that familiar, still, small voice kept whispering, "Alex, TRUST Me. I've never let you down. I will be with you this time, too."

I wanted to believe that voice, the reassuring voice of the Lord. But about one week before the conference, I drove to my bank to arrange for a loan to cover the financial shortfall I was *sure* we'd have. (See, I'm really a spiritual wimp.)

Sitting in the bank parking lot, I felt kind of ashamed. Did I really believe that God could make this succeed against what looked like impossible odds? I swallowed hard, said a prayer, and drove away from the bank without ever going in.

My staff and I called everyone we knew to promote the event. We didn't have any funds left for radio and newspaper ads. It was now a matter of prayer and word-of-mouth promotion.

The day before the event, we had 1,000 people
signed up. Our speakers ar-
Jesus + relationship   rived at the local airport,
= eternal life   and we were on our way. I
went to bed praying for the
event, and I was still awake
as the first light of day appeared.

Ready or not, the "Truth for a New Generation"
event was about to begin.

To be continued . . .

TRUST GOD WHEN LIFE GETS WEIRD

The book of Hebrews offers some can't-miss en-
couragement when life gets weird:

> Let us throw off everything that hinders
> and the sin that so easily entangles, and let
> us run with perseverance the race marked
> out for us. Let us fix our eyes on Jesus, the
> author and perfecter of our faith, who for
> the joy set before him endured the cross,
> scorning its shame, and sat down at the
> right hand of the throne of God. Consider
> him who endured such opposition from sin-
> ful men, so that you will not grow weary
> and lose heart. (12:1-3)

Jesus overcame death on the cross so that
through His power, each one of us can overcome
the obstacles that stand in our way . . . regardless of
how hopeless the situation may seem.

This realization has made a difference in my own walk with Christ.

And through the years I've discovered what Joseph knew: I'm not alone when I face hardships. I've learned that every Christian, at one time or another, wrestles with trials and fears . . . even feelings of inadequacy. It's the same for you. As a young man or woman who is heading down the road to eternal life, keep in mind that life is more often hard than easy.

But pressing on, as Joseph did, is the key. And consider this: Jesus overcame death and the struggles of this world just for you and me. He headed down a road that took Him to His physical death. But He also walked down a spiritual road that led to life.

When troubles hit, remind yourself of these truths:

1. We're connected to our Creator. You know what the Messiah did nearly 2,000 years ago—He came into the world, died on a cross, was resurrected, then ascended into heaven. And you know what that means for all who commit their lives to Him—*salvation* (eternal life), *liberation* (freedom for the captives), and *restoration* (healing of the brokenhearted).

2. We're on a mission of living out our faith . . . and telling the world what and Who anchors our lives.

3. We must trust *God's Words when life feels hopeless:*

> Christ died for sins once for all, the righteous
> for the unrighteous, to bring you to God.
> (1 Peter 3:18)

God so loved the world that he gave his one
and only Son, that whoever believes in him
shall not perish but have eternal life. (John
3:16)

Jesus said, "Peace be with you! As the Father
has sent me, I am sending you." And with that
he breathed on them and said, "Receive the
Holy Spirit." (John 20:21-22)

This is love for God: to obey his commands.
And his commands are not burdensome, for
everyone born of God overcomes the world.
(1 John 5:3-4)

*4. We must praise God at all times . . . hard and
happy.* Consider this prayer of praise by Saint
Francis of Assisi:

You are holy, Lord, the only God,
and Your deeds are wonderful.
You are strong.
You are great.
You are the Most High.
You are Almighty.
You, Holy Father, are King of heaven and earth.
You are Three and One, Lord God, all Good.
You are Good, all Good, supreme Good, Lord God,
    living and true.
You are love. You are wisdom.
You are humility. You are endurance.

You are rest.

You are peace.

You are joy and gladness.

You are justice and moderation.

You are all our riches, and You suffice for us.

You are beauty.

You are gentleness.

You are our protector.

You are our guardian and defender.

You are our courage. You are our haven and our
hope.

You are our faith, our great consolation.

You are our eternal life, Great and Wonderful
Lord,

God Almighty, Merciful Savior.[3]

SERVICE

A model inmate
Genesis 40

As time goes by, Pharaoh's chief cupbearer and baker offended their master. The king of Egypt is so furious with the two that he puts them in custody under the captain of the guard. It's the same jail where Joseph is being held.

The warden assigns Joseph to attend to their needs.

Weeks and months pass, and on one particular night, the cupbearer and the baker both have dreams. Each dream is very curious and haunts the two men.

When Joseph arrives in the morning, he notices that they're feeling low. So he asks them, "What's wrong? Why the long faces?"

Both men share what happened in the night: "We dreamed dreams and there's no one to interpret them."

Joseph studies them for a moment and then asks, "Don't interpretations come from God? Tell me your dreams."

The chief cupbearer speaks first: "In my dream, I saw a vine in front of me, and on the vine were three branches. As soon as it budded, it blossomed, and its clusters ripened into grapes. Pharaoh's cup was in my hand, and I took the grapes, squeezed them into Pharaoh's cup, and put the cup in his hand."

Joseph unlocks the mysteries of the dream, saying, "Here's the meaning: The three branches are three days. Within three days, Pharaoh will get you out of here and put you back to your old work—you'll be giving Pharaoh his cup just as you used to do when you were his cupbearer. Only remember me when things are going well with you again—tell Pharaoh about me, and get me out of this place. I was kidnapped from the land of the Hebrews. And since I've been here, I've done nothing to deserve being put in this hole."

Next, the baker shares his dream, but Joseph's words for him are anything but favorable. In fact, his interpretation is downright gruesome!

"The three baskets are three days," Joseph tells him. "Within three days Pharaoh will take off your head and impale you on a tree, and then the birds will pick your bones clean."

Sure enough, events happen just as Joseph had predicted. But for two years, the chief cupbearer doesn't gives Joseph another thought.[1]

Exactly who were the king's chief cupbearer and baker? Their humble titles don't fully communicate the responsibilities of these two men. First, the baker was probably in charge of all Pharaoh's food. By comparison in today's world, he'd be more like the food-service manager in the White House. This was an important job in the king's palace operations.

Likewise, the cupbearer tasted all the king's food and drink. In other words, he was in charge of the king's security. Imagine his job as being the head of the White House security detail.

These were very big jobs, and it was a dramatic and significant turn of events for both of these men to end up in prison.

Joseph befriended these guys, and from what happened next, it was obvious that he knew them well enough to detect when they were in a bad mood. One day the two servants appeared to be "dejected" (Genesis 40:6). Joseph asked them, "Why are your faces so sad today?"

Think about it: Even though Joseph was terribly mistreated, he maintained a humble spirit and a tender heart. Anyone locked away in an Egyptian prison had a right to be sad. Yet Joseph had the ability to shine even in the most miserable of conditions. His leadership ability was so obvious that he was even put in charge of the people he was locked up with (39:22).

The cupbearer and the baker could have answered, "Joseph, you fool, why aren't *you* sad? Look around you: We're in prison!"

Instead, the two men described their dreams, and Joseph showed them kindness. What's more, Joseph exercised an amazing gift: his ability to interpret dreams. (It eventually led to his pardon.)

Many people, when they've been wronged, put on calm facades. They describe their situation as "no big deal" or claim they've "gotten over it." But in reality they've hardened their hearts. They've forced themselves not to have feelings or emotions for the people or situations in their past.

How can it be that Joseph remained so free of bitterness? Clearly his heart hadn't hardened. I think it's because he never lost his faith in God. Through it all, he trusted in God's sovereignty, in God's ability to deliver him when the time was right, and in God's love—a love that Joseph believed would work good both in his own life and in the lives of those he loved.

Happiness and moral duty are inseparably connected.
—George Washington

The bottom line is this: Joseph reached out to others and remained faithful even when he was betrayed or in difficult circumstances. He knew that God would work all things out for the good of others—and for his own well-being.

He was a true servant-leader.

The Ephesians 3:19 secret

when jesus christ rules your life, you have love that surpasses knowledge, and you're "filled to the measure of all the fullness of god" (ephesians 3:19). but what exactly does this mean?

- when you face the impossible, god does the impossible. (luke 18:27)
- when it's hard to express love, god fills you with his unconditional love. (romans 5:5; 1 john 4:7, 19)
- when you just don't know how to pray, the holy spirit guides you. (romans 8:26)
- when you're weak, christ fills you with his strength. (2 corinthians 12:9-10)
- when circumstances overwhelm you, god's infinite wisdom is available to you. (james 1:5)

SPIRITUAL "WAIT" TRAINING: GOD'S TIMING IS PERFECT

It may take a period of patient waiting before God speaks to us about an issue—a hope, a dream, a goal. Why? Because He has forgotten or because it's not that important to Him? Absolutely *not*! It's because in the process of making us wait, He is preparing us for His answer, which we may have missed had He spoken to us immediately. The Lord won't tell us some things instantaneously. Sometimes we have to wait a season of time—at least until we're prepared to listen. These times may draw out and stretch our faith, but as Henry Blackaby points out,

The interpretation of dreams—Joseph style!

Dreams were a frequent mode of God's revelation in the Old Testament. Take a look at these verses:
- Genesis 28:12
- Genesis 31:10-11
- Genesis 37:5-9
- Genesis 40:5
- Genesis 41:1
- Numbers 12:6
- Judges 7:13
- 1 Kings 3:5
- Daniel 2:3
- Daniel 4:5
- Daniel 7:1

He will take whatever time is necessary to grow your character to match His assignment for you.... Character-building can be long and painful. It took 25 years before God entrusted Abraham with his first son and set in motion the establishment of the nation of Israel. Yet God was true to His Word.[2]

SERVE GOD RIGHT WHERE YOU ARE

Okay, you may not have the power to interpret dreams, but you do have gifts to share. It's Christ in you and the outpouring of His love through your words, your warmth, and your walk that will impact humanity for Him. It's *Jesus' face* reflected in your face that will open others' eyes to the possibility that there is a God. Are you sharing God's love with those around you? What do people see when they look at your life? Humility, kindness, goodness—a reflection of Christ's face?

Consider these words of Jesus as your "stimulus package" toward a secure spiritual future:

> Then the King will say to those on his right, "Come, you who are blessed by my Father; take your inheritance, the kingdom prepared for you since the creation of the world. For I was hungry and you gave me something to eat, I was thirsty and you gave me something to drink, I was a stranger and you invited me in, I needed clothes and you clothed me, I was sick and you looked after me, I was in prison and you came to visit me." (Matthew 25:34-36)

One reason I love history is because it offers wonderful role models as inspiration to do well in life. There's a well-known legend that in the eleventh century, the Bavarian duke known as Henry III decided that he was tired of being a political figurehead and leader. So he applied to join a local monastery, where he planned to spend the rest of his life in solitude and spiritual reflection.

The leader of the monastery responded to the Duke's request for entry: "Your Majesty," Prior Richard began, "do you understand that the pledge here is one of obedience? That will be hard because you have been a king."

Henry replied, "I understand. The rest of my life I will be obedient to you, as Christ leads you."

Hearing the Duke's pledge of obedience, the wise Prior Richard said, "Then I will tell you what to do. Go back to your throne and serve faithfully in the place where God has put you."

In the Bible, love often refers to action—stuff we do rather than stuff we feel.

Henry III did exactly what he was told. After he died, a statement was written: "The King learned to rule by being obedient."

Joseph knew this too.

It's a lesson Henry III learned, and it's one that we can apply to our own lives: Accept life's challenges as growth exercises that Christ expects us to handle faithfully.

SEEK WAYS TO SERVE GOD

As Christians, and as people who call ourselves servants of God, we're supposed to engage people with love. It's not just about going on a mission trip to Mexico. It's about the community that you live in and the places where you spend your time. In other words, be a missionary in *your hometown.*

I like what Christian scholar Oswald Chambers wrote on this subject. Take a look:

Has it ever dawned on you that you are responsible for other souls spiritually before God? For instance, if I allow any private deflection from God in my life, everyone about me suffers. . . . When once you allow physical selfishness, mental slovenliness, moral obtuseness, spiritual density, everyone belonging to your crowd will suffer. "But," you say, "who is sufficient for these things if you erect a standard like that?" Our sufficiency is of God, and of Him alone.[3]

Need some ideas on how to serve God? Need to get out of your protective box? As Christians, sometimes we have this picture that as long as we stay in a safe box, life will be perfect. Yet God calls us as a church to get out of our boxes. He wants us to engage the world for Him.

In other words, tell your story:

- Explain what you're all about and what Christ is all about.
- Let your actions speak love.
- Do something you might not normally do: Show kindness to a stranger—maybe a homeless guy or some neighborhood kids whose parents desperately need a break.

You can also show simple acts of kindness. Help a friend clean up his or her room, take out the trash, or help with his or her homework. Invite someone to church or youth group. Show someone that you love him or her through your actions, not just with your words.

Finally, you can serve God by striving to be an encourager. The world needs encouragers—godly people who offer kindness and compassion, faithful "Joseph types" who are willing to reach out to those who have been wounded by discouragers. Ask the Lord to show you how to be merciful, just as He is merciful. Consider this: God reaches out to the unlovable, befriends those the world would rather forget, and touches those who seem untouchable.

WISDOM

called to pharaoh's court
Genesis 41:1-40

Joseph, now 30 years old, is thin and pale from the years he spent in the dark prison, yet he still carries himself with a confident stride. And today he's holding his head especially high. Joseph is standing before the most powerful man in Egypt: Pharaoh himself.

The king regards the slave, who nods and smiles.

"I had a dream," Pharaoh tells Joseph, "and no one can interpret it. But I have heard it said of you that when you hear a dream you can interpret it."

"I cannot do it," Joseph replies, "but God will give Pharaoh the answer he desires."

After the ruler has shared his dream with Joseph, the Hebrew ponders what he has heard. Then Joseph's expression grows solemn and his voice is soft with humility and perfect certitude: "Pharaoh's two dreams both mean the same thing.

The way of wisdom

James 1:5 says, "But if any of you lacks wisdom, let him ask of God, who gives to all generously and without reproach, and it will be given to him" (NASB). And Proverbs 2:6 tells us, "For the Lord gives wisdom; from His mouth come knowledge and understanding" (NKJV). When the Bible speaks of wisdom, it means much more than intelligence and the ability to score a 1,400 on the SAT. Biblical wisdom is about walking obediently with God and applying His truth to our lives. Here are two key ways to become wise:

1. Ask Jesus to help you disconnect from the world's lies and learn to stand firmly in His truth. "There's a way that seems right to a man, but in the end it leads to death" (Proverbs 14:12).

2. Evaluate your weak points, and then take action. "Let us throw off everything that hinders . . . and let us run with perseverance the race marked out for us" (Hebrews 12:1).

God is telling Pharaoh what he is going to do. The seven healthy cows are seven years and the seven healthy ears of grain are seven years—they're the same dream, seven years of plenty. The seven sick and ugly cows that followed them up are seven years and seven scrawny ears of grain dried out by the east wind are the same—seven years of famine."

Joseph advises Pharaoh to store a portion of the food produced in the seven good years to prepare for the seven difficult years that will follow.

Pharaoh is so pleased with Joseph's counsel that he declares, "Since God has made all this known to you, there is no one so discerning and wise as you.

You shall be in charge of my palace, and all my people are to submit to your orders. Only with respect to the throne will I be greater than you."[1]

Scripture doesn't tell us how Joseph behaved or what he thought during the next two years, but we can assume that once again he acquitted himself with honor.

Even though Joseph had every reason to sulk and feel sorry for himself, what happened next indicates that, to the contrary, Joseph behaved in a way that prepared him for leadership, not pity.

At the end of those two years, Pharaoh himself had dreams. Then and only then did the cupbearer remember Joseph's ability to interpret dreams. It's interesting to speculate as to why the cupbearer remembered Joseph only then. Some commentators suggest that the cupbearer was trying to make himself look good in Pharaoh's eyes, hoping to appear as a problem solver.

Others say that the cupbearer was showing true repentance. After all, the cupbearer says, "Today I am reminded of my shortcomings. Pharaoh was once angry with his servants, and he imprisoned me" (Genesis 41:9-10). In other words, the cupbearer wanted to forget that episode in his life, but Pharaoh's dreams forced him to face his broken promise to Joseph.

After hearing from the cupbearer, Pharaoh quickly summoned Joseph. "Pharaoh said to Joseph, . . . 'I

have heard it said of you that when you hear a
dream you can interpret it'" (verse 15).

Joseph immediately gave God the credit for any
gift of interpretation he had. "'I cannot do it,'
Joseph replied to Pharaoh, 'but God will give
Pharaoh the answer he desires.'"

This is both a humble and risky answer. Pharaoh
and Joseph, after all, don't worship the same God.
For Joseph to so directly testify to God's power
couldn't be interpreted as anything but an affront
to Pharaoh and his power. But it was a risk that
Joseph took, and God blessed his humility.

Joseph said that both dreams were the same.
They were just two different ways of saying, or seeing, the same thing: Seven years of abundance
would be followed by seven years of famine. Joseph
said that the famine would be so severe that it
would take a "discerning and wise man" to take
charge of all of Egypt (verse 33). The excess from
the seven good years would be needed during the
seven years of famine, and the storage operation
would be massive.

Joseph laid out a sophisticated and clever plan
for Pharaoh so that Egypt wouldn't be "ruined by
the famine" (verse 36).

Pharaoh, though, knew that he had his man
standing before him. Joseph, after all, had come up
with the plan. Joseph had heard God's voice and had
proven his ability to work diligently, even in difficult circumstances.

We don't know if these conversations took place

in a matter of minutes or over several hours or even days. Scripture seems to suggest they happened very quickly. The point is clear: Joseph's moment had come.

Wisdom is the ability to see future consequences of present actions.

He had spent half his life either in prison or as a slave. But because Joseph hadn't wallowed in pity, because he had diligently done his best in all that he attempted, and because he kept an open ear and heart to hear God's voice and wisdom, he was ready when his God and his king called him to a vital duty.

GOD'S WORD IS TRUSTWORTHY AND TRUE

God's Word is relevant and absolutely, positively accurate in everything God felt was essential for us to know. Scripture contains God's very words and offers solid advice for just about every situation you'll ever encounter. Through the Bible God teaches, rebukes, corrects, and trains us in righteousness. These ancient words are amazingly timeless: "All Scripture is God-breathed and is useful for teaching, rebuking, correcting and training in righteousness, so that the man of God may be thoroughly equipped for every good work" (2 Timothy 3:16-17).

Joseph gave credit where credit was due: the eternal wisdom of the one and only Lord of the universe. Joseph's humility brings to mind the faith of another godly man.

Christians in the crossfire

The border between North and South Korea–
called the 38th parallel–is a deadly war zone.
It's a place where ideologies clash and armed
soldiers stand ready for battle 24/7. Just as those
countries are in conflict, we're in the middle of a
war every day over what's real, what's meaning-
ful, and what's true. As christians living in the
world, we're literally caught in the middle. But
God has given us an important mission: He's
counting on us to show others what truth is and
how it's relevant to our lives today. How can you
fulfill this mission in your sphere of influence?
By letting your faith shine through your actions
and showing your friends the source of hope and
joy in your life. Don't be afraid to speak up. Tell

In the late 1800s Dwight L. Moody was America's
most well-known minister and was loved by people
around the world. Because of his solid stand for
Christianity and his loyalty to the Bible, Moody was
a frequent target of criticism by the atheists of the
day. In modern times, famous atheists such as
Richard Dawkins and Christopher Hitchens have
made a career of trying to disprove Christianity.
Such skeptics were around a century and a half ago
as well.

Moody was once asked if he really believed that
God caused a great fish to swallow Jonah. "Of
course," Moody said. He reasoned, "The book of
Jonah says that God *prepared* a great fish to swallow Jonah. If God could create this world, couldn't

them about your worldview: what's real and what's worth living for. Tell them about your convictions and certain choices you've made—and why you made them. Consider this advice from C. S. Lewis:

> As Christians we are tempted to make unnecessary concessions to those outside the faith. We give in too much. Now, I don't mean that we should run the risk of making a nuisance of ourselves by witnessing at improper times, but there comes a time when we must show that we disagree. We must show our Christian colours, if we are to be true to Jesus Christ. We cannot remain silent or concede everything away.[2]

God make a fish large enough to swallow Jonah? If He chose, God could prepare a man large enough to swallow a whale!"[3]

Though Moody's response to the skeptic may sound extreme, his reasoning was correct. An *a fortiori* argument is reasoning "from the greater to the lesser." For example, if a weight lifter could bench-press a 250-pound barbell, chances are that he could pick up a 30-pound box filled with copies of this book.

I don't read the Bible because I'm a great saint. I read it because I'll find God there.
—Rich Mullins

So, is it reasonable to believe the miracle stories in your Bible? Of course!

Think about it. If God could create the universe, then causing a fish to swallow Jonah would be no problem. If God could create the entire human race, could He raise a dead body back to life? Yes. Since He clearly has done the greater, it's obvious that He could do the lesser.

GROW WISE THROUGH PRAYER AND BIBLE STUDY

It's obvious that Joseph spent time with his heavenly Father, strengthening his relationship with God and growing spiritually wise. Even though Scripture doesn't give examples of Joseph praying to God, it's safe to assume that he had a vital, vigorous prayer life. How do we know this? (1) We read many examples of God speaking to Joseph through dreams; (2) Joseph grows into a wise interpreter of dreams; and (3) the Bible refers to Joseph's dreams—and his ability to interpret them—as gifts from God.

It's essential that you, too, strive to grow spiritually wise. Have a daily quiet time with God and make an effort to . . .

- seek Him with a spirit of submission
- get on your knees in prayer
- study Scripture
- just be still before the Lord, listening to Him

Contemporary Christian artist Keith Green recorded a song called "Make My Life a Prayer to You." I believe that song and Joseph's life point us in the right direction. Time alone with God is vital, and the result of that time alone should be a humble heart and a life of obedience.

Here's how you can apply Joseph's example to your life:

1. Begin your quiet time with prayer. The Bible is so foundational to our faith. Unfortunately, it can also seem so foundational that it's almost dry. To help battle this feeling, consistently spend time in prayer before you read God's Word. Read Scripture with a prayerful heart and ask God to minister to you through His message. Ask Him to remove the distractions that keep you from knowing Him better. When you sit down to read and your heart isn't prepared, you can miss a message God may have for you.

Pray something like this: "Heavenly Father, make me hungry for Your Word and thirsty for time with You. Build in me a strong, healthy faith. Amen."

2. Commit Scripture to memory. In addition to reading the Bible, get in the habit of memorizing verses. The more Scripture you get into your head, the stronger you'll grow spiritually. Here's a verse to consider memorizing: "The word of God is living and active. Sharper than any double-edged sword, it penetrates even to dividing soul and spirit, joints and marrow; it judges the thoughts and attitudes of the heart" (Hebrews 4:12).

3. Study in SPACE. Consider using the acronym SPACE when you study Scripture. With this method, you can ask yourself questions pertaining to a passage you're reading.

S—Is there a *Sin* I need to confess?

P—Is there a *Promise* I need to claim?

A—Is there an *Attitude* I need to change?

C—Is there a *Commitment* I need to make?

E—Is there an *Example* I need to follow?

When you ask yourself these questions, one of them will often apply to your life.

4. Pray continually. Scripture tells us to "pray without ceasing" (1 Thessalonians 5:17, KJV). If the only prayer that counts is the time when our eyes are closed and our knees are bowed, then God has given us a command that's impossible to obey. I don't believe He would do that. Pray several times throughout the day—for big things and small things. Thank God for His many blessings in your life and tell Him how much you love Him.

Consider Thomas à Kempis's prayer for wisdom:

Grant me, O Lord, to know what is worth knowing, to love what is worth loving, to praise what delights You most, to value what is precious in Your sight, to hate what is offensive to You. Do not let me judge by what I see, nor pass sentence according to what I hear, but to judge rightly between things that differ and above all to search out and to do what pleases You, through Jesus Christ our Lord.[4]

BLESSING

earthly rags to eternal riches
Genesis 41:41–57

Pharaoh tells Joseph, "I hereby put you in charge of the whole land of Egypt."

Then the king removes his signet ring from his finger and slips it on Joseph's finger. He dresses Joseph in robes of fine linen and puts a gold chain around his neck. Then the king puts the second-in-command chariot at Joseph's disposal, and as the Hebrew rides throughout the land, people shout, "Bravo!"

Joseph, the son of Jacob, now has the power to issue orders in the king's name and the ring to seal his commandments. He is no longer a slave and a prisoner. He is now a new governor with a new name: *Zaphenath-Paneah,* which means "God Speaks and He Lives." His fame goes forth throughout Egypt, as well as into the kingdoms north and east.

Pharaoh also gives Joseph an Egyptian wife, Asenath, the daughter of Potiphera, the priest of On (Heliopolis).

As the king's right-hand man, Joseph takes up his duties over the land of Egypt.[1]

Joseph had to end up in Egypt as a servant to Pharaoh. But why not just give Joseph the equivalent of an Old Testament MBA and send him to an Egyptian executive training program? Why not let him rise up through the ranks comfortably? Wouldn't that have accomplished the same thing without all that hardship and pain? Obviously, God didn't think so.

First, Joseph was a gifted but proud young man. That pride had to be refined out of him in the furnace of hardship and humiliation.

Second, Joseph's brothers were jealous of him. They had to be brought to a point of submission so they, too, would accept the help that Joseph, through Pharaoh, would offer.

Of all the blessings of heaven, one of the greatest will be you!
—Max Lucado, Grace for the Moment

Third, the drought and worldwide famine taught the nations that trusting God is the only sure way to peace and security.

Not only did God have a unique plan, but the story itself unfolded in ways that were necessary for the ultimate fulfillment of that plan.

The only path to heaven: two truths

Truth No. 1: Don't try to earn your way into heaven. It just can't be done. Nothing you do, including "good" works, can protect you from the burning flame of God's holiness. "All our righteous acts are like filthy rags; we all shrivel up like a leaf, and like the wind our sins sweep us away" (Isaiah 64:6). Truth No. 2: Trust Christ and what He accomplished by His death and resurrection. This is the one true path to eternity.

While Joseph's life seemed to be moving from one form of enslavement to the next, from one unthinkable challenge to another, God was in control and blessed Joseph—and future generations.

YOUR LIFE CAN MAKE A DIFFERENCE

When Tricia Brock of Superchic was in high school, she made a decision to lay down her life for Christ and for her friends. "It was hard," she says. "All around me were different cliques. Kids seemed to hide in them. Some of the cliques looked out for themselves and stepped on whoever they could in order to climb the popularity ladder."

Yet Tricia remembers a few teens who really tried to make a difference in the lives of others—not by going around preaching big sermons but by *living* their faith and *walking* their talk.

"Those were the kids who I wanted to be like," Tricia adds. "I made an effort to love every person

Count your blessings

sometime soon, grab a sheet of paper and go off to a quiet place. At the top of the sheet, write "Blessings from God." Spend some time reflecting on your life and all that you're thankful for--especially how the Lord has been with you during tough times. Next, write a prayer to Jesus, counting your blessings and thanking God for His presence in your life.

I met, whether it was the guy on worship team or the girl at school who was the slacker and into drugs. I did my best to see people the way God sees them. I remember saying to myself, 'I'm making this decision right now that I don't care if I'm popular, and I don't even care if I get picked on for doing these things.' I learned that when you stand up for what you believe, people will begin to respect you. They'll notice that there's something bigger in your life that you live for."[2]

That "something bigger" is God's will.

A TEST OF MY FAITH, PART 2

God's will is revealed when we seek Him. He has already mapped out our lives since birth. But it's entirely up to Him when He decides to make His presence and power directly known to us. And once this happens, our lives are forever changed. God's Word tells us, "Commit to the LORD whatever you do, and your plans will succeed" (Proverbs 16:3).

Here's the rest of the story about the "Truth for a New Generation" event. But first, a recap: The "Truth for a New Generation" apologetics event was about to begin. But had I heard God correctly? Should I have spent my entire savings to rent a 5,000-seat convention center when it looked as if only 1,000 people were planning to attend?

As I drove up to the conference venue early that morning, I couldn't believe my eyes. The line of people stretched around the building and down the block!

School buses rolled up, and the line of cars seemed like it went for miles. People were walking to the convention center from all directions. I sat in my car, overcome with emotion, and thanked God for what I was seeing.

By 9:00 AM, as the event got underway, the coliseum's turnstiles had recorded that 4,701 people had entered the building. I was amazed, my staff was ecstatic . . . and Mr. Moradian was on cloud nine!

Our prayers had been answered, and the event was a major success. God had come through just as He said He would.

This test of faith was a major turning point in my life as well. The magnitude of this single conference set in motion a chain of events that brought other significant opportunities into my life. The process of planning the event taught me to trust God, not to play it safe. I suppose I passed the test, but only barely. True, I didn't downsize, even though an "expert" encouraged me to do so. I *did* follow what I thought God wanted me to do, but my heart was trembling the entire time!

I believe that if I hadn't followed the Holy Spirit's leading in this assignment, if I hadn't done what God required of me, I doubt that I would have caught the attention of Focus on the Family. And if I had failed at this key point in my life, I don't believe I would have been given the opportunities to write books, become a seminary president, or experience countless other blessings from God. The Lord had to know that I was willing to trust Him.

Not one person on this planet is beyond God's reach.

Our Creator is faithful, and I can testify to that fact! This event is only one example. When you face a faith test, are you able to trust God? Can you obey Him, even when it stretches your faith? Trust me—blessings follow when we stand firm in God's promises.

CHOOSE GOD'S DEFINITION OF SUCCESS

God views success differently than the world does. He doesn't look at your IQ or how many friends you have on Facebook. God doesn't care what kind of car you drive, how big your house is, or even if you own a platinum credit card with no spending limit. All the power, money, and fame in the world doesn't impress God the least bit.

So, exactly how does He want you and me to re-define success?

As Joseph discovered, success in God's eyes means you must be willing to give up everything—yourself, your possessions, your pride, your power—in order to gain what God has in store for you. It's sometimes true that in doing so you may never achieve what you always dreamed of. But when you fully surrender your life to God, He often returns those dreams and talents to you. One thing is always true: God's plans for you are bigger, grander, and more wild than you could ever imagine.

Take a few clues from Joseph's success secrets:

- Never say, "God, this is what *I* want." Instead, ask, "God, what do *You* want?"
- Never say, "God, I *won't . . .*" Instead, always say, "God, I'll do *Your* will."
- Never look for self-satisfaction. Instead, seek to satisfy God.
- Never seek the approval of people. Instead, seek God's approval.
- Never measure success by how well things are going. Instead, measure success by a life centered in God's will.
- Never put your own needs first. Instead, always think of others first.
- Never look to your own capabilities to solve a problem. Instead, rely fully on God's power to lead you.

FORGIVENESS

rivalry revisited
Genesis 43:1–45:15

Joseph feels as if he's about to explode.

He has pretended long enough. The cup in Benjamin's sack was the last test. Now he knows that Judah and the others had not betrayed another son of Rachel. The older brothers have changed.

He turns to his attendants and cries out in Egyptian, "Leave! Clear out—everyone leave at once!"

With only his brothers in the room, he is free to reveal his true identity. Yet the pent-up emotion inside is too much to control. Tears roll down Joseph's cheeks, and his breath is squeezed in his chest. He weeps so loudly, people hear him throughout the house. Joseph's brothers stand with their mouths ajar, speechless, with terror and guilt and wonder.

Then the grand vizier of Egypt kneels down in front of his brother Judah. He speaks to him in Hebrew: "It's me—your brother."

He stands up and goes to Benjamin. "I am Joseph," he says.

"Reuben," he sobs, "look at me. Simeon, I am your brother. Levi, look closely at me. I'm not dead. Dan! Asher! Gad! Naphtali—it's me, Joseph. Is it true? Is my father really still alive?"

His brothers, still stunned by the scene, don't say a word. They simply cannot believe what they are hearing and seeing.

"Come to me," Joseph says with a motion.

They move closer to him and peer into his eyes. Joseph nods his head. "Yes, I am Joseph your brother whom you sold into slavery," he tells them. "And now, do not be distressed and do not be angry with yourselves for selling me here, because it was to save lives that God sent me ahead of you. For two years now there has been famine in the land, and for the next five years there will not be plowing and reaping. But God sent me ahead of you to preserve for you a remnant on earth and to save your lives by a great deliverance."

Joseph hugs his brothers one by one and holds them tightly until all of the men are weeping.

They make plans to bring Jacob and the rest of their family to Egypt.[1]

It's one of Scripture's great ironic twists. The same brothers who had sold Joseph into slavery were now powerless before him, begging for a handout. They were literally at the mercy of the man they had once plotted to kill.

How could Joseph be so forgiving?

Answer: He fully trusted in God's sovereignty. God had used Joseph's circumstances—even his years in slavery and prison—to bring about the salvation of his father's family—a family that would eventually bring to the world the Messiah.

Imagine if Joseph had simply been the lord of his brothers during a lifetime in Canaan. They would have tolerated each other, perhaps, but the brothers would have continued in their envy and jealousy, and it's possible that the family would have been completely destroyed both spiritually and physically when the famine hit. What happened instead is this: Jacob's family experienced a spiritual and physical healing. The brothers repented and were reconciled not just to Joseph but to Jacob, their father, and to God, their heavenly Father.

But the most incredible part was Joseph's reaction to them: He shed tears of love and compassion, not bitterness. Despite years of mistreatment, he had grown into a strong man—big enough to forgive his brothers, and understanding enough to see God working through his circumstances.

What's more, the dream that set in motion Joseph's wild odyssey was coming to pass. As a teen Joseph had angered his brothers by telling them about his vision: "We were binding sheaves of grain out in the field when suddenly my sheaf rose and stood upright, while your sheaves gathered around mine and bowed down to it" (Genesis 37:7).

When Joseph's brothers stood face-to-face with their now grown-up brother, they had no idea who he was. And Joseph didn't reveal his identity at first or let on that he knew who they were. In fact, he had them arrested as spies and, on the third day, told them, "If you are honest men, let one of your brothers stay here in prison, while the rest of you go and take grain back for your starving households. But you must bring your youngest brother to me, so that your words may be verified and that you may not die" (42:19-20).

So, as a test, Joseph held Simeon as hostage.

It's tempting to think that Joseph was inflicting a cruel trick on his brothers. But a closer look reveals that he was being both wise and compassionate. To begin with, Joseph had no way of knowing the true character of these guys. Since they suddenly showed up in Egypt, claiming they were seeking food for starving households, he wanted to make certain that their intentions were honorable. Did they truly care about others, or were they just looking out for themselves?

What's more, nearly 20 years had passed, and the last time he had seen them, they were up to some pretty ugly antics: (1) They sold Joseph into slavery and, in all likelihood, an early death; (2) they betrayed their father; and (3) their hearts were hardened with anger and cruelty. Had these guys changed?

But something bigger was at work here. God was using Joseph to bring his brothers to repentance. As the men prepared to leave Joseph, they said to one another, "Surely we are being punished because of our brother. We saw how distressed he was when he

A believer's five-point call to compassion

1. A believer is called to help those in need. (Acts 2:44-45)
2. A believer is called to love. (Romans 13:8)
3. A believer is called to support those in ministry. (1 Corinthians 9:14; 3 John 5-8)
4. A believer is called to set a good example. (1 Timothy 4:12; Titus 2:7)
5. A believer is called to serve. (1 Peter 4:10)

pleaded with us for his life, but we would not listen; that's why this distress has come upon us" (42:21).

When Joseph revealed himself to his brothers, God revealed Himself to both Joseph and the brothers in this way: They all realized that everything had happened for a divine purpose. Joseph had been placed in a position of authority to preserve the Hebrews in a time of famine. And it would be through Jacob's family— through Judah himself— that the line of David, and eventually Jesus Himself, would come.

> *Impressed by their bold belief, he said, "Friend, I forgive your sins." (Luke 5:20, MSG)*

Together, Joseph and his brothers moved through the healing steps of forgiveness and restoration. Genesis 45:1-15 paints one of the Bible's most intensely emotional scenes and sets an example for us to follow.

Forgiven and free

Colossians 3:13 tells us how to be forgiven and free: "Bear with each other and forgive whatever grievances you may have against one another. Forgive as the Lord forgave you." First, accept God's forgiveness. When you've blown it in some way, go to the Lord in prayer. Confess your sin, ask for forgiveness, and press ahead in the power of the Lord.

Second, learn from your mistakes. It's every Christian's responsibility to practice avoiding the traps that cause you to stumble.

Third, forgive others. Has somebody wronged you? Are you harboring bitterness? Don't delay. Go to that person and strive to work through the problem. Above all, forgive as God has forgiven you.

GOD FREES US FROM BONDAGE

The Holy Spirit gives us the wisdom to make good decisions, along with the strength to carry them out. Saturate your mind with Scripture, pray, rely on God's strength when you're weak, seek the kind of joy that can only come from a hope in heaven—not from the things of this world. The bottom line is this: Value what Jesus values. He will free you from bondage and guide you along a path that leads to purpose and meaning in life—that is, if you let Him. Consider this advice from the apostle Paul:

> Be very careful, then, how you live—not as unwise but as wise, making the most of every opportunity, because the days are evil. Therefore

do not be foolish, but understand what the
Lord's will is. Do not get drunk on wine, which
leads to debauchery. Instead, be filled with the
Spirit. (Ephesians 5:15-18)

An unforgiving heart can erect giant, ugly walls
between us, our friends, and our family—even our
God. Joseph knew this. And so did my dad.

One of the greatest lessons I ever learned was
when my father and I battled one of those ugly
walls together.

I gripped a sledgehammer like a baseball bat,
held it high over my shoulder, and then swung with
all my might. *SMACK!* The sledgehammer connected with a cement wall—and nearly knocked me
to the ground. I looked up and groaned.

"It's hopeless, Dad," I said with frustration in my
voice. "There's no way this thing is coming down."

My father was much more optimistic. "Put your
back into it, get angry, and aim for a stress point.
Nail the sweet spot, and I'm tellin' you, Son, this
thing's history!"

What began as a *weekend* project turned into
weeks of muscle-aching, backbreaking labor. Dad
wanted to expand the basement of our North Carolina
home, but a stubborn wall stood in his way—a bar-
rier that I'm guessing was built thousands of years
ago by a master Egyptian craftsman. Like the ancient pyramids, it stood the test of time.

Get angry, huh? I told myself. *This wall's no
match for a McFarland. It's gravel bait!* I let loose

with another mean swing, and this time . . . I managed to fall on my backside. I kicked the hammer. "Forget it, Dad. This is a waste of time."

My father picked up the tool, stared intently at the wall, then swung. *CRACK!* With a single skillful connection, the wall broke into a thousand dusty pieces.

My mouth dropped open, and I gasped. Dad looked at me with a wink and said, "It's all about the stress points."

In my relationships through the years, I've learned to look for those stress points in myself and in others, and to do business with them right away. Ephesians 4:26-27 tells us, " 'In your anger, do not sin': Do not let the sun go down while you are still angry, and do not give the devil a foothold."

And verses 31-32 give us instructions on how to live: "Get rid of all bitterness, rage and anger, brawling and slander, along with every form of malice. Be kind and compassionate to one another, forgiving each other, just as in Christ God forgave you."

Henri Nouwen, one of Christianity's amazing thinkers, paints a beautiful picture of our call as believers to forgive, love, and lay down our lives for others. Take a look:

> After washing His disciples' feet, Jesus says,
> "I have given you an example so that you may
> copy what I have done to you" (John 13:15).
> After giving Himself as food and drink, he
> says, "Do this in remembrance of me" (Luke

22:19). Jesus calls us to continue His mission of revealing the perfect love of God in this world. He calls us to total self-giving. He does not want us to keep anything for ourselves. Rather, He wants our love to be as full, as radical, and as complete as His own. He wants us to bend ourselves to the ground and touch the places in each other that most need washing. He also wants us to say to each other, "Eat of me and drink of me." By this complete mutual nurturing, He wants us to become one body and one spirit, united by the love of God.[2]

LEARN TO FORGIVE

Take the healing steps that restored Joseph's family:

1. Allow God to work out forgiveness *in your heart.* In fact, Christ forgives as we forgive others. Take a good hard look at Matthew 6:14-15. Our Savior's words in these verses are tough—and may even make your knees weak. He tells us that our Father will not forgive our sins if we don't forgive those who sin against us. Search your heart: Is there any darkness or resentment that you'll be held accountable for before God?

You have a Friend who sees in you what other people sometimes miss. (Read John 15:9-15 for a clue.)

2. Know that God's nature is forgiveness. (Check out Exodus 34:6-7.) As sinners we're all "children of wrath" and "strangers" to God's promises (Ephesians 2:3, 12, NASB). Yet the Lord forgave our rebellion against Him (verses 4-10). And even while we were still rejecting God, Romans 5:8 says that Jesus died for us. Get this: Christ looked down at those who nailed Him to a cross and cried out, "Father, forgive them, for they do not know what they are doing" (Luke 23:34).

3. *Deal with anger and bitterness.* Unsure about what to do when you're feeling angry and bitter? Try this:

- Shift your focus away from the emotion and concentrate on dealing with the situation as Jesus would.
- Pray, asking God for help in those volatile moments.
- Strive to settle whatever has you angry. When you sit and stew about a situation, the whole thing can grow bigger than it has to be. The wise thing to do if you're angry is to deal with it—quickly.

PROVIDENCE

Joseph, Jesus, and you!
Genesis 46:28–47:31

Joseph goes to Pharaoh and tells him all about his family's big move south: "My father and brothers with their flocks and herds and everything they own have come from Canaan. Right now they are in Goshen."

Joseph goes to Goshen in his chariot to meet his father. The moment Joseph sees Jacob, he throws himself on his father's neck and weeps for a long time.

Jacob says to his son, "I'm ready to die. I've looked into your face—you are indeed alive."

Then Joseph takes five of his brothers with him and introduces them to Pharaoh.

"Your servants are shepherds, the same as our fathers were. We have come to this country to find a new place to live. There is no pasture for our flocks in Canaan. The famine has been very bad

there. Please, would you let your servants settle in
the region of Goshen?"

Pharaoh looks at Joseph. "Your father and your
brothers have come to you, and the land of Egypt is
before you; settle your father and your brothers in
the best part of the land. Let them live in Goshen.
And if you know of any among them with special
ability, put them in charge of my own livestock."

Joseph brings his father, Jacob, in and presents
him to Pharaoh. Jacob blesses the king, then
Pharaoh asks, "How old are you?"

Jacob says, "The years of my pilgrimage are a
hundred and thirty. My years have been few and difficult, and they do not equal the years of the pilgrimage of my fathers."

Jacob blesses Pharaoh again, and then he leaves
the king's presence.

Joseph settles his father and his brothers in
Egypt and gives them property in the best part of
the land, the district of Rameses.

Jacob lives in Egypt 17 years with his family before he dies at the age of 147.[1]

If one sentence could summarize Joseph's life, it
would be this: Amazing good came from unthinkable evil.

Joseph was terribly mistreated by his brothers.
Yet God used their evil actions not only to save others but even to save their own lives and the lives of
their families (see Genesis 45:4-8). Think about

Have faith in God's providence

In his book "The Sovereign God," James Montgomery Boice wrote:

> The providence of God does not relieve us of responsibility. God works through means (the integrity, hard work, obedience and faithfulness of Christian people, for example). The providence of God does not relieve us of the need to make wise judgments or to be prudent. On the other hand, it does relieve us of anxiety in God's service. (See Matthew 6:30.) Rather than a cause for self-indulgence, compromise, rebellion or any other sin, the doctrine of providence is actually a sure ground for trust and a spur to faithfulness (emphasis added).[2]

this: *Joseph's brothers were saved by the one they rejected!* This faithful patriarch reminds us of a much greater man who changed human history: Jesus Christ.

Like Joseph, the Lord was rejected by those He came to save. Think about these sobering thoughts by Bible scholar and author Calvin Miller:

> As Jesus' cry of loneliness faded into stillness, there was nothing but the whisper of afternoon breeze and the scream of the carrion eagles, circling in the sickly sky above the tree. But Jesus' tormentors were wrong in their conclusions. There is always a time when the silence ends. There is always a time when God answers evil![3]

Theologians call Joseph a "type" of Jesus. That doesn't mean he was Jesus, or even a manifestation of Jesus. But Joseph wasn't God; he was just a man. Since he was a man who had so completely given himself over to being God's servant, his character resembled that of Jesus.

One of the ways Joseph's life points us toward Christ is through events that symbolized the resurrection of Jesus. Joseph, in different ways, became dead to his family, to his homeland, and even to his vocation as a landowner. He was thrown into a pit by his brothers and into prison by Potiphar. But in these spiritual graveyards, Joseph defeated despair and ultimately emerged triumphant. Joseph didn't literally, or physically, rise from the dead, but it's easy to see how God used these events in Joseph's life to provide foreshadowing for the future life, death, and resurrection of Jesus.

> *To be Christian is to be reborn, and free, and unafraid, and immortally young.*
> *—Joy Davidman, wife of C. S. Lewis,* Smoke on the Mountain

All the seemingly meaningless and tragic elements of Joseph's life were really part of a grand plan to save an entire race of people. Even Joseph seemed to have a sense of that grand plan while he was in the middle of it. It is in this respect—sensing God's bigger plan—that Joseph was most like Jesus.

Attempting to discover God's plan for our own lives should be what we strive for from the exam-

ple of Joseph, and from the life of Jesus. The most
important lesson we can learn from Joseph's life is
that God is in control. He is continually directing
the affairs of humankind and the events of history
toward a particular goal: to bring glory to Himself.

God doesn't exist for our pleasure; we're created
for *His* pleasure.

THE HEART OF SALVATION

The idea that God's goodness and severity could be
two sides of the same coin came to me when many
years ago I met a man named Sheldon Vanauken.

At the time I was a graduate student at Liberty
University in Lynchburg, Virginia, and Vanauken
was a patient of my wife, who was a nurse. I soon
learned that Vanauken had known C. S. Lewis.
When Vanauken's wife, Davy, died of a mysterious
disease, Lewis wrote letters of comfort to Vanauken,
saying that Davy's death was a severe blow, but one
day Vanauken might come to see it as a part of
God's plan, a part of God's mercy. Vanauken eventually wrote a book, *A Severe Mercy,* about his and
Davy's conversion, their life together, and Davy's
eventual death.

Of course, Vanauken would never have chosen
death for his wife. Yet her passing resulted in a
book that has now been read by millions of people—
and has led to the conversion of millions to Christianity. It was a lasting legacy of both his and Davy's
years together. Vanauken's testimony reminds us

Snapshots of Joseph

- The book of Genesis dedicates the final 14 chapters (Genesis 37-50) to the life of Joseph. That's one-quarter of the book! Both in terms of his strategic positioning at the beginning of the Bible and the amount of time dedicated to him, Joseph is one of the most important characters in the Bible.

- Hebrews 11, the chapter often called the Hall of Faith, mentions Joseph along with Abraham, Isaac, Jacob, Moses, Rahab, and Noah. This is a very short list of some of the most faithful men and women in all of history—and Joseph is on it (see verse 22).

- From the very beginning of recorded religious history, Joseph was recognized as an important figure. In the ancient Jewish rabbinical tradition, there are more midrashic (teaching,

all that God is good, even when His mercies seem severe.

As I studied Vanauken's journey, I was reminded of Lewis's experiences, especially his insight into suffering.

After spending most of his life as a bachelor, he fell in love with and married a woman named Joy Davidman, even though he knew she was dying of cancer. Some might call the love story ironic or tragic, and in some ways it was both. Yet the fruit of that relationship resulted in some of Lewis's most moving writing, especially his books *A Grief Observed* and *The Four Loves*, works that some critics have suggested Lewis couldn't have written if or homiletic) narratives about Joseph than about anyone else in biblical history. Joseph is also a central figure in Islam. He is considered an Islamic prophet and an ideal man. In many Islamic countries, calling a man a "second Joseph" is to say that he is extraordinarily handsome and has an exemplary character.

- Consider our own fascination with Joseph today: The Broadway play "Joseph and the Amazing Technicolor Dreamcoat" is based on the Life of Joseph. It has been performed continuously since its debut in the 1970s. The 1995 television mini-series "The Bible: Joseph" won an Emmy that year. And the great twentieth-century novelist Thomas Mann devoted four novels to the Life of Joseph and his brothers.

he hadn't found love himself. Here is an excerpt from *The Four Loves*, published in 1960, just months after Joy's death:

> To love at all is to be vulnerable. Love anything, and your heart will certainly be wrung and possibly be broken. If you want to make sure of keeping it intact, you must give your heart to no one, not even to an animal. Wrap it carefully 'round, with hobbies and little luxuries; avoid all entanglements; lock it up safe in the casket or coffin of your own selfishness. But in that casket—safe, dark, motionless, airless—it will change. It will not be broken;

it will become unbreakable, impenetrable, ir-
redeemable. The only place outside Heaven,
where you can be perfectly safe from all the
dangers of love . . . is Hell.[4]

I don't know about you, but on most days I don't
feel I have either the intellectual firepower of a
C. S. Lewis or the spiritual depth of Jesus. In fact,
I'd say that's true *every* day.
That's why I take comfort
in this verse, which seems
to be written just for me:
"Though a righteous man
falls seven times, he rises again" (Proverbs 24:16).

The word providence
*literally means "to
see beforehand."*

SEEK GOD'S BLESSING FOR THE SAKE OF OTHERS

At the end of Jacob's life, he blessed his sons and
summarized Joseph's life:

> Joseph is a fruitful vine,
>   a fruitful vine near a spring,
>   whose branches climb over a wall.
> With bitterness archers attacked him;
>   they shot at him with hostility.
> But his bow remained steady,
>   his strong arms stayed limber,
> because of the hand of the Mighty One of Jacob,
>   because of the Shepherd, the Rock of
>   Israel. (Genesis 49:22-24)

What was true for Joseph can be true for you

Trusting God isn't easy, especially when we don't understand what He's doing. Joseph probably felt the same way, but he continued trusting God for the outcome of his life. When you feel as if you're walking in the dark, and nothing makes sense, don't give up. Trust in God's providence . . .

- when you feel overwhelmed, remember: God cares about you.
- when you don't understand, remember: God does have a plan.
- when you can't see a solution, remember: God is at work.
- when you've done wrong, remember: God restores those who repent.
- when you've been wronged, remember: God can work it out for your good.

In spite of what happened to Joseph, he remained steady and confident in the Lord. Because he was willing to trust God with his life, God used him in powerful ways. Like Joseph, we must be *willing*—willing to follow, willing to be uncomfortable, and above all, willing to risk everything.

How about you? Will you risk all for God?

Don't hide behind an excuse: "Who, me? I don't know what to say. I'm not smart enough or strong enough to do the job. Pick someone else." You've heard the excuses before. Maybe you've used them yourself. But God doesn't tolerate an excuse. (Just ask Joseph!)

We all want our lives to count. The question is

this: Are you willing to let your life count for God so that you can be a blessing to others?

If you are, here are some steps you can take toward that goal:

1. Focus your heart on the truth. Christians believe in right and wrong and that God's truth is ultimate and unchanging. Joseph took God at His word and didn't falter. As the Creator of all, the Alpha and the Omega "who is, and who was, and who is to come, the Almighty" (Revelation 1:8), God is Truth—*absolute Truth.* Or, as C. S. Lewis explains in his book *Mere Christianity*, God is the Mind and the Power behind the Moral Law of the Universe:

> It is after you have realized that there is a real
> Moral Law, and a Power behind the law, and
> that you have broken that law and put yourself
> wrong with that Power—it is after all this, and
> not a moment sooner, that Christianity begins
> to talk.[5]

2. Be willing to leave your comfort zone. A comfort zone is a selfish, protective cocoon that keeps us from being all God wants us to be. But get this: Clinging to a comfortable life can end up killing the soul. So be willing to step out of your comfort zone and trust God. The farther away from your comfort zone that you are, the more you'll experience His comfort. Paradoxical but true! God used Joseph more when he was outside his homeland than when he was in it.

3. Pursue God's call on your life with a whole heart. You'll make mistakes, and others may try to stand in your way. But the best thing you can do is strive to be humble and teachable. Be confident, too. Like Joseph, get up when you fall and keep moving forward.

4. Forgive. Here's an old saying: "Holding on to anger is like drinking poison and expecting the other person to die." Forgiving is a gift to yourself, and it furthers God's kingdom. That's why Jesus instructed us to pray and to forgive:

> "Our Father in heaven, hallowed be your name,
> your kingdom come, your will be done on
> earth as it is in heaven. Give us today our daily
> bread. Forgive us our debts, as we also have
> forgiven our debtors. And lead us not into
> temptation, but deliver us from the evil one."
> For if you forgive men when they sin against
> you, your heavenly Father will also forgive
> you. But if you do not forgive men their sins,
> your Father will not forgive your sins.[6]

The shining hallmark of Joseph's character is that he was able to forgive his brothers who tried to kill him (Genesis 45:5-15). Jesus forgave those who did kill Him (Luke 23:34).

Experts and skillful people do things that set them apart from the rest of the pack. Malcolm Gladwell, in his book *Outliers*, tells how experts become experts. He talks about musicians, sports figures, and business leaders who went on to become great because of their commitment. Citing examples such as the Beatles, Bill Gates, and Tiger Woods, Gladwell concludes that it takes 10,000 hours of practice to become an expert. But, if an intense period of focused attention and practice occurs, Gladwell believes people can achieve excellence in a shorter time. He compares it to the pressure that turns carbon into coal and then into diamonds.[7]

I believe that God can use the pressure and challenges we go through to make us stronger as well. Just as Joseph overcame disappointments and struggles to become a great leader for God, you, too, have an opportunity to rise above your circumstances. There will be times in life when you feel as if the pain and struggles are just too much to bear. But there is no easy path to greatness. Experts, leaders, and spiritual champions are produced only through commitment. You may think to yourself, *Another wound, another burden, one more blow, and I am going to die!* But God whispers: "Trust me. I have not left you. I am with you." And like Joseph of old you will find that your obedience to God and your commitment to His call have purified, strengthened, and refined you. You have become a champion for God.

FORTY PARALLELS BETWEEN JOSEPH AND JESUS

This list is not intended to prove that Joseph was a prototype of Jesus, but it does note some significant similarities between their lives. (And some not-so-significant ones too.) The parallels are not merely coincidence. The lives of Joseph and Jesus clearly point out that God's Way is full of twists and turns, angst and anguish. And yet it's also full of peace, hope, and miraculously good endings.

JOSEPH

1. Joseph's father, Jacob, gave Joseph authority. (Genesis 37:2)

2. Joseph was a shepherd. (Genesis 37:2)

3. Jacob loved Joseph. (Genesis 37:3)

4. Jacob elevated Joseph's status. (Genesis 37:3-4)

5. Joseph was hated without cause by his brothers. (Genesis 37:4)

6. Joseph predicted through a God-given dream that he would have great status and be worshiped. (Genesis 37:7-9)

7. Jacob sent Joseph to his brothers. (Genesis 37:13)

8. Joseph's brothers conspired and plotted against him. (Genesis 37:18-20)

9. Joseph's brothers stripped off his clothing. (Genesis 37:23)

10. Joseph was placed in a hole in the earth. (Genesis 37:24)

11. Gentile travelers came to Joseph from the East (Gilead), with spices, balm, and gold. (Genesis 37:25)

12. Joseph was betrayed for the price of a slave, 20 pieces of silver. (Genesis 37:28)

JESUS

1. The heavenly Father gave Jesus authority.
   (Matthew 22:44; 28:18; 1 Peter 3:22)
2. Jesus called Himself "the Good Shepherd."
   (John 10:14)
3. The heavenly Father loved Jesus.
   (Matthew 3:17; Mark 1:11; Luke 3:22; John 17:23)
4. The heavenly Father elevated Jesus' status:
   "Therefore God exalted him to the highest
   place." (Philippians 2:9)
5. Jesus was hated without cause.
   (John 15:18)
6. God predicted through Scripture that Jesus
   would have great status and be worshiped.
   (Isaiah 45:23-24)
7. The heavenly Father sent Jesus into the
   world. (John 17:18)
8. The rulers of the Jews conspired and plotted
   against Jesus. (Mark 3:6; John 11:53)
9. Soldiers stripped off Jesus' clothing.
   (John 19:23)
10. Jesus was placed in a hole in the rock.
    (Matthew 27:60; Mark 15:46; Luke 23:53;
    John 19:41)
11. Gentile travelers came to Jesus from the East
    (Babylon) with spices (frankincense), balm
    (myrrh), and gold. (Matthew 2:1-12)
12. Jesus was betrayed for 30 pieces of silver,
    which was the price of a slave in that day.
    (Matthew 26:14-15; Exodus 21:32; see also
    Zechariah 11:12)

JOSEPH

13. Joseph emerged alive from an intended grave. (Genesis 37:28)

14. Gentile traders took Joseph to Egypt. (Genesis 37:28)
15. Jacob tore his clothes in mourning for Joseph. (Genesis 37:34-35)
16. Joseph found favor with people. (Genesis 39:2, 6)
17. Joseph was tempted to sin by a devilish woman, yet he overcame. (Genesis 39:7)

18. Joseph was falsely accused of a crime. (Genesis 39:14-19)
19. Joseph was arrested for a crime he did not commit. (Genesis 39:20)

20. The Egyptian jailer looked favorably on Joseph. (Genesis 39:21-23)

21. Joseph was innocent, yet he was placed with two offenders. (Genesis 40:1-4)

22. Joseph accurately predicted the destiny of two men. (Genesis 40:12-22)

23. Joseph ministered to ungrateful people. (Genesis 40:23)

JESUS

13. Jesus emerged alive from an intended grave: "He is not here; he has risen!" (Matthew 28:6; Luke 24:6)

14. Jesus' earthly parents (Joseph and Mary) took Him to Egypt. (Matthew 2:13-15)

15. The heavenly Father tore the temple curtain when Jesus died. (Matthew 27:45-46, 51)

16. Jesus found favor with God and people. (Luke 2:52)

17. Jesus was tempted to sin by the devil, yet He overcame. (Matthew 4:1-11; Mark 1:12-13; Luke 4:1-13)

18. Jesus was falsely accused of wrongdoings. (Matthew 27:12; Luke 11:14-15)

19. Jesus was arrested for crimes He did not commit. (Matthew 26:47-56; Mark 14:43-52; Luke 22:47-53; John 18:2-12)

20. The Roman centurion looked favorably on Jesus: "Surely he was the Son of God!" (Matthew 27:54)

21. Jesus was innocent, yet He was placed between two thieves. (Matthew 27:38; Mark 15:27)

22. Jesus accurately predicted the destiny of a thief: "Today you will be with me in paradise." (Luke 23:43)

23. Jesus ministered to ungrateful people: "Where are the other nine?" (Luke 17:17; 17:11-18)

JOSEPH

24. Joseph was summoned by leaders.
    (Genesis 41:14)

25. Joseph was given power and authority by
    Pharaoh. (Genesis Genesis 41:39-44)

26. Joseph traveled in royal style. (Genesis 41:43)

27. Every knee bowed to Joseph. (Genesis 41:43)

28. Joseph began public service at age 30.
    (Genesis 41:46)

29. Joseph gathered a harvest of grain that could
    not be counted. (Genesis 41:49)

30. Pharaoh told the people to obey Joseph.
    (Genesis 41:55)

31. With God's help, Joseph offered the only
    source of life-giving bread in a worldwide
    famine. (Genesis 41:56)

32. Joseph's blessings from God were first recog-
    nized by nonfamily members. (Genesis 41:37-
    46, 57)

33. Joseph's brothers suffered for their plot
    against Joseph. (Genesis 42:21)

34. Joseph wept over the actions of those he
    loved. (Genesis 42:24)

35. Joseph demanded total surrender from his
    brothers to prove they were authentic.
    (Genesis 42:34)

JESUS

24. Jesus was summoned by leaders. (Matthew 26:57-68; 27:11; Mark 14:53-65; 15:1-6; Luke 22:66–23:12; John 18:12, 19-24)

25. Jesus was given power and authority by God. (Isaiah 53:12; Matthew 7:29; Mark 1:22; 1 Corinthians 15:24-28)

26. Jesus will return in royal splendor. (Matthew 26:64; Luke 21:27; Revelation 19:11-16)

27. Every knee will bow to Jesus. (Philippians 2:10)

28. Jesus began public ministry at age 30. (Luke 3:23)

29. Jesus will gather a harvest of souls that cannot be counted. (Revelation 7:9-10)

30. Jesus' mother told the people to obey Jesus. (John 2:5)

31. Jesus is "the bread of life." (John 6:35; see also 6:31-51)

32. Jesus' blessings from God were first recognized by nonfamily members. (Mark 7:24-30; Luke 7:1-10; Romans 15:8-13)

33. Jews suffered for their plot against Jesus. (Matthew 23:38; Luke 13:35)

34. Jesus "beheld the city, and wept over it." (Luke 19:41-44, KJV)

35. Jesus demanded total surrender from His disciples to prove they were authentic. (Matthew 10:37-39; 16:24-25)

JOSEPH

36. Joseph invited those he loved to a banquet. (Genesis 43:16)

37. Joseph showed himself alive to his family. (Genesis 45:3-4)

38. Joseph explains his mission, extends forgiveness, and dispels fears. (Genesis 45:5-6, 15)

39. Joseph was acknowledged as a ruler or king by relatives, the family of Jacob (Israel). (Genesis 45:26)

40. Joseph protected his family during the worldwide famine. (Genesis 45–47)

JESUS

36. Jesus had a banquet or feast with His disciples at the Last Supper. (Mark 14:12-26). He also used a banquet story to symbolize heaven, where loved ones will gather. (Luke 14:12-24)

37. Jesus "showed himself . . . and gave many convincing proofs that he was alive" to the disciples. (Acts 1:3; see also Luke 24:39)

38. Jesus explains His mission, extends forgiveness, and dispels fears. (Matthew 28:9-10; Luke 24:17-47)

39. Jesus was acknowledged as a king by the family of Jacob, which is Israel. (Matthew 21:1-11)

40. Jesus will protect His people. (Revelation 7:15)

A GENESIS READING GUIDE

finding God's way

What comes next in this sequence: J, F, M, A, _? The answer is M. Why? Let me fill in the missing information for you. January, February, March, April, *M*ay.

Now, what's next in this sequence: M, T, W, T, _? This time I hope the answer was easier for you to see. It's F for Friday.

A good part of life is recognizing patterns. When we study the Bible, we learn to recognize God's Way—His pattern. The book of Genesis offers the beginnings of many patterns. It's the stirring prologue of God's great story: the creation of all things, the origin of humanity, and God's original blueprint for this world. Without Genesis your understanding of the story will be incomplete. Without Genesis, you wouldn't be able to recognize and understand His complete pattern.

The pattern and ways of Joseph point to Jesus (see "Forty Parallels Between Joseph and Jesus"), who really is the Beginning and End of the pattern.

If you want to learn God's Ways, a good start is to read His Words. Use the following journal space to record what you've learned about God and how His followers should live by studying the life of Joseph.

Genesis 37

_____

_____

_____

_____

_____

Genesis 38

_____

_____

_____

_____

Genesis 39

_____

_____

_____

_____

_____

Genesis 40

_____

_____

_____

_____

_____

Genesis 41

_____

_____

_____

_____

Genesis 42

_____

_____

_____

_____

_____

Genesis 43

_____

_____

_____

_____

_____

Genesis 44

_____

_____

_____

_____

Genesis 45

_____

_____

_____

_____

_____

Genesis 46

_____

_____

_____

_____

_____

Genesis 47

_____

_____

_____

_____

_____

Genesis 48

_____

_____

_____

_____

_____

_____

Genesis 49

_____

_____

_____

_____

_____

Genesis 50

_____

_____

_____

_____

_____

NOTES

Introduction

1. Napoleon Hill, quoted in Max Lucado, *Grace for the Moment* (Nashville: J. Countryman, 2000), 215.
2. C. S. Lewis, *Mere Christianity* (New York: Macmillan, 1952), 43.

Chapter 1

1. Biblical accounts of Joseph's life in the opening section of this chapter have been adapted and paraphrased from the *New International Version* and *The Message*.

Chapter 2

1. C. S. Lewis, *The Problem of Pain* (New York: Macmillan, 1962), 93.
2. Charles H. Spurgeon, quoted in Calvin Miller, ed., *The Book of Jesus* (New York: Simon and Schuster, 2005), 467.
3. Henry Blackaby, Blackaby Ministries International, "Be Anxious for Nothing," February 8, 2009, http://www.blackaby.org/devarchive.asp (accessed April 15, 2009).

Chapter 3

1. Story adapted and paraphrased from Genesis 39:1–6, MSG.

2. A. W. Tozer, *Tozer on Christian Leadership: A 366-Day Devotional* (Camp Hill, PA: Christian Publications, 2001), reading for October 19.
3. Saint Augustine, quoted in Jonathan Aitken, *Prayers for People Under Pressure* (New York: Continuum International Publishing Group, 2006), 116.

Chapter 4

1. Story adapted and paraphrased from Genesis 39:7-19, NIV.
2. Interview with the author, September 12-14, 2008, Camp Tadmor, Lebanon, Ore.
3. Dietrich Bonhoeffer, *The Cost of Discipleship* (New York: Macmillan, 1963), 47-48.

Chapter 5

1. Story adapted and paraphrased from Genesis 39:20-23, NIV and MSG.
2. C. S. Lewis, *Letters of C. S. Lewis* (New York: Macmillan, 1966), 220.
3. Saint Francis of Assisi, "Prayer in Praise of God, Given to Brother Leo," quoted in National Shrine of Saint Francis of Assisi, "Franciscan Prayers," http://www.shrinesf .org/prayers.htm (accessed April 15, 2009).

Chapter 6

1. Story adapted and paraphrased from Genesis 40, NIV and MSG.

2. Henry T. Blackaby, *Experiencing God Day-by-Day* (Nashville: Broadman and Holman, 1998), 16.

3. Oswald Chambers, *My Utmost for His Highest* (New York: Dodd, Mead and Company, 1935), 46.

Chapter 7

1. Story adapted and paraphrased from Genesis 41:1-40, NIV and MSG.

2. C. S. Lewis, *God in the Dock* (Grand Rapids: Eerdmans, 1970), 262.

3. D. L. Moody, *Pleasure and Profit in Bible Study* (Chicago: Revell, 1895), 21.

4. Thomas à Kempis, quoted in Dorothy M. Stewart, *The Westminster Collection of Christian Prayers* (Louisville, KY: Westminster John Knox Press, 2002), 369.

Chapter 8

1. Story adapted and paraphrased from Genesis 41:41-57, NIV and MSG.

2. Tricia Brock, Superchic, interview by contributing writer Michael Ross, October 2002.

Chapter 9

1. Story adapted and paraphrased from Genesis 43:1–45:15, NIV and MSG.

2. Henri J. M. Nouwen, *Show Me the Way* (New York: Crossroad Publishing, 1995), 130-31.

Chapter 10

1. Story adapted and paraphrased from Genesis 46:28–47:31, NIV and MSG.
2. James Montgomery Boice, *The Sovereign God: Foundations of the Christian Faith* (Downers Grove, IL: InterVarsity, 1979), 235.
3. Calvin Miller, *Once Upon a Tree* (West Monroe, LA: Howard Publishing, 2002), 47.
4. C. S. Lewis, *The Four Loves* (New York: Harcourt Brace Jovanovich, 1960), 169.
5. C. S. Lewis, *Mere Christianity* (San Francisco: HarperCollins, 1952), 27.
6. Matthew 6:9-14
7. Malcolm Gladwell, *Outliers* (New York: Little, Brown, and Company, 2008), 35-67.